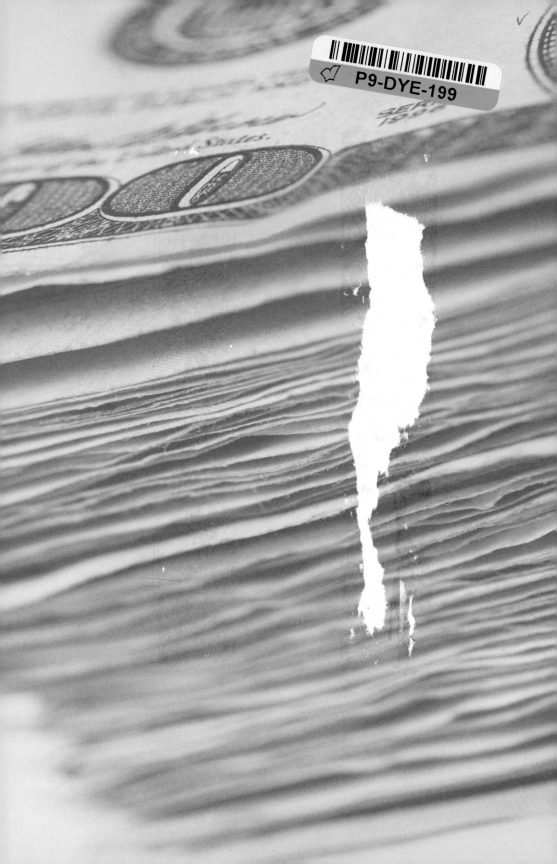

Yes, You Can SUPERCHARGE YOUR Portfolio!

Also by Ben Stein

HOW SUCCESSFUL PEOPLE WIN: Using "Bunkhouse Logic"
to Get What You Want in Life

HOW TO RUIN YOUR FINANCIAL LIFE

HOW TO RUIN YOUR LIFE (hardcover)
(also available as an audio book)

HOW TO RUIN YOUR LOVE LIFE

HOW TO RUIN YOUR LIFE tradepaper (comprises the three titles above)

HOW YOU CAN SELL ANYONE ANYTHING (co-written with Barron Thomas)
(available May 2008)

THE REAL STARS: In Today's America, Who Are the True Heroes?

26 STEPS TO SUCCEED IN HOLLYWOOD . . . or Any Other Business
(co-written with Al Burton)

Also by Ben Stein and Phil DeMuth

CAN AMERICA SURVIVE?: The Rage of the Left, the Truth, and What to Do about It

YES, YOU CAN BE A SUCCESSFUL INCOME INVESTOR!:
Reaching for Yield in Today's Market

YES, YOU CAN GET A FINANCIAL LIFE!: Your Lifetime Guide to Financial Planning

YES, YOU CAN STILL RETIRE COMFORTABLY!:
The Baby-Boom Retirement Crisis and How to Beat It

All of the above are available at your local bookstore, or may be ordered
by visiting the distributors for New Beginnings Press:

Hay House USA: **www.hayhouse.com**®
Hay House Australia: **www.hayhouse.com.au**
Hay House UK: **www.hayhouse.co.uk**
Hay House South Africa: **www.hayhouse.co.za**
Hay House India: **www.hayhouse.co.in**

Yes, You Can SUPERCHARGE YOUR *Portfolio!*

Six Steps for Investing Success in the 21st Century

BEN STEIN AND PHIL DeMUTH

NBP

NEW BEGINNINGS PRESS
Carlsbad, California

Published by: New Beginnings Press, Carlsbad, California

Distributed in the United States by: Hay House, Inc.: www.hayhouse.com • *Distributed in Australia by:* Hay House Australia Pty. Ltd.: www.hayhouse.com.au • *Distributed in the United Kingdom by:* Hay House UK, Ltd.: www.hayhouse.co.uk • *Distributed in the Republic of South Africa by:* Hay House SA (Pty), Ltd. • www.hayhouse.co.za • *Distributed in Canada by:* Raincoast: www.raincoast.com • *Distributed in India by:* Hay House Publishers India: www.hayhouse.co.in

Editorial supervision: Jill Kramer   *Design:* Tricia Breidenthal

Library of Congress Cataloging-in-Publication Data

Stein, Benjamin.
  Yes, you can supercharge your portfolio! : six steps for investing success in the 21st century / Ben Stein and Phil DeMuth. -- 1st ed.
     p. cm.
  Includes index.
  ISBN 978-1-4019-1763-0 (hardcover) -- ISBN 978-1-4019-1764-7 (tradepaper) 1. Finance, Personal--United States. 2. Investments--United States. 3. Financial security--United States. I. DeMuth, Phil, 1950- II. Title.
HG179.S58315 2008
332.6--dc22   2007014431

Hardcover ISBN: 978-1-4019-1763-0
Tradepaper ISBN: 978-1-4019-1764-7

11 10 09 08   4 3 2 1
1st edition, January 2008

Printed in the United States of America

Contents

Introduction

In July 2003, Ben Stein (one of your authors) was invited on *Jimmy Kimmel Live* to compete in a stock market portfolio grudge match with Kimmel's own Tad ("Big Tad") Newcomb. The idea was that each of them would carefully select five stocks, and then they would see whose portfolio performed better.

In some ways, it was not really a fair fight. Ben Stein knows an enormous amount about finance, while Tad is not what you'd call a deep thinker in this department. More than a few pounds overweight, Tad spends his days watching TV. His self-professed life goal is "to get a girl to have sex with me." Still, *The Wall Street Journal* has routinely shown portfolios created by throwing darts that made monkeys out of Wall Street's best and brightest.

These were Ben's and Tad's picks:

Ben's List

- Templeton Emerging Markets Income Fund, Inc. (ticker: TEI)
- Cohen & Steers Realty Majors (ICF)
- S&P Depository Receipts (SPY)
- Diamonds Trust (DIA)
- Boeing (BA)

A word of explanation, so you can play along at home: The Templeton Emerging Markets Income Fund owns a basket of bonds (debt) from developing countries like India, Brazil, Russia, and so on. Cohen & Steers Realty Majors is a collection of real estate investment trusts, which are companies that own commercial real estate such as shopping centers, office buildings, hotels, and apartment buildings. The S&P Depository Receipts owns a sampling of all of the companies in the S&P 500 Index and is a proxy for tracking the performance of that stock index of America's largest companies. The Diamonds Trust has nothing to do with a girl's best friend, but instead owns the 30 blue chip stocks that compose the Dow Jones Industrial Average. Boeing is the single example of an individual stock pick on Ben's list: They make airplanes.

Tad's list was different:

Tad's List

- Playboy Enterprises, Inc. (PLA)

- Krispy Kreme Doughnut Corp. (KKD)

- Harley-Davidson, Inc. (HOG)

- Anheuser-Busch Companies, Inc. (BUD)

- TiVo, Inc. (TIVO)

Tad's picks require little in the way of further explanation—like tongue sandwiches, they speak for themselves. We might say that Tad is developing an investment "theme" here, based on eating, drinking, and making merry. Considering the importance of the pleasure principle in human affairs, these are probably reliable bets. Notably, one of his stock picks—Anheuser-Busch—is also a favorite of world-class heavyweight investor Warren Buffett, although we're not certain that Tad consulted Warren in making his selection (or vice versa).

Who won the competition? Ben and Tad went back on the show two months later to see whose portfolio was bigger. Here's how they fared:

Ben's List

- Templeton Emerging Markets Income Fund, Inc. (TEI) +4.6%

- Cohen & Steers Realty Majors (ICF) +5.1%

- Standard and Poor's Depository Receipts (SPY) +2.7%

- Diamonds Trust (DIA) +4.2%

- Boeing Co. (BA) +7.3%

Tad's List

- Playboy Enterprises, Inc. (PLA) +10%

- Krispy Kreme Doughnut Corp. (KKD) -6.7%

- Harley-Davidson, Inc. (HOG) +5.1%

- Anheuser-Busch Companies, Inc. (BUD) -2.8%

- TiVo, Inc. (TIVO) -4.9%

Ben's average two-month total return was 4.8 percent, compared with Tad's total return of 0.1 percent. While Tad's Playboy looked promising (a bet on the continuing appeal of large bosoms, although we only read it for the articles), he was dragged down by beer, doughnuts, and TV. In a strange way, this seemed like a metaphor for Tad's personal situation.

The long-term results are even more skewed. This was the situation three years later:

Ben's List

- Templeton Emerging Markets Income Fund, Inc. (TEI) +37.4%

- Cohen & Steers Realty Majors (ICF) +125.9%

- Standard and Poor's Depository Receipts (SPY) +39.7%

- Diamonds Trust (DIA) +32.9%

- Boeing Co. (BA) +142.9%

Tad's List

- Playboy Enterprises, Inc. (PLA) -30.0%

- Krispy Kreme Doughnut Corp. (KKD) -81.0%

- Harley-Davidson, Inc. (HOG) +26.8%

- Anheuser-Busch Companies, Inc. (BUD) -3.3%

- TiVo, Inc. (TIVO) -22.7%

Ben's portfolio is up 76 percent—nearly twice the increase of the market as a whole and comparing quite favorably with Tad's, which is down 22 percent. Tad's best pick (Harley-Davidson, up 26.8 percent) isn't even up as much as Ben's worst pick (the Diamonds Trust, up 32.9 percent).

Now Tad is a very likable fellow, even if he does have trouble getting a date on Saturday night. His investing theme seemed completely bankable, anchored in the constants of human nature. But something seems to have gone very, very wrong.

Perhaps you are a bit like Tad, at least in this one respect. You have some good investing ideas, and yet at the end of the day, the quarter, or the year, they don't seem to have panned out quite the way you hoped. This kind of thing happens all the time. Sometimes it seems like the stock market was invented to make us crazy and to teach us bone-crunching lessons in humility.

This book is going to show you how to take your portfolio and transform it from the lovable but ill-fated Tad's into the Pentium-powered Ben Stein's. What's more, this is going to be easier than you think. By the time you've finished, it's going to seem like so much common sense.

As was the case in our other investing classics (which you should run out and purchase immediately), we will have occasion to mention a Website or two along the way. We will provide you with links to all of these from the Stein-DeMuth Website (**www.stein-demuth.com**), which is the only one you need to bookmark. There we will also bring you any updates to this book that we think you might find useful, as well as correct any errors that may have crept into our otherwise immortal prose.

Over the years, we've seen a lot of people's investment portfolios, and most of what we've observed isn't pretty. This holds true even for high-net-worth investors. There's just an astonishing amount of bad investment advice floating around. If you've fallen victim to it, you've got plenty of company. That's the bad news.

The good news is that you can do better. In most cases, there are comparatively simple steps you can take to supercharge your portfolio. We're going to show you how.

Chapter One

Step 1: Don't Skip Step 1

What do you think of the investment portfolio shown in Figure 1?

Figure 1.1: A Five-Star Fund Portfolio

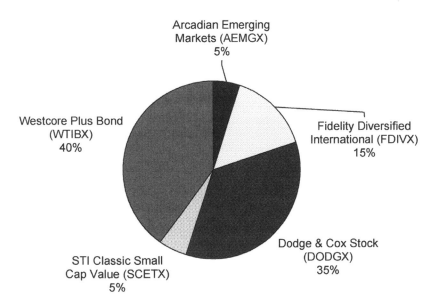

Arcadian Emerging
Markets (AEMGX)
5%

Fidelity Diversified
International (FDIVX)
15%

Westcore Plus Bond
(WTIBX)
40%

Dodge & Cox Stock
(DODGX)
35%

STI Classic Small
Cap Value (SCETX)
5%

Let us quickly point out that these mutual funds have all been given the highest possible rating (five stars) by Morningstar, the premier mutual fund rating agency. The portfolio is allocated along conventional lines, with 40 percent in intermediate-term bonds and 60 percent in stocks. Furthermore, 20 percent is invested abroad. The portfolio has some hot market segments, including a nominal exposure to emerging markets and domestic small cap value stocks. In short, there's a great deal to admire here.

However, as you probably expected, we have no particular reason to recommend this portfolio. It's just a MacGuffin—it leads nowhere, necessarily. It might be catastrophic or it might be the cat's pajamas. With so much seemingly going for it, what makes us hesitate? Step 1.

Step 1: Evaluate Your Needs
Before Deciding on Your Investments

Starting with the investment selection process is like looking through the wrong end of the rifle. Portfolios don't exist in the abstract; they're created in some context, to fulfill some human purpose. The type of portfolio you should hold depends on what you're trying to accomplish.

This sounds so trivially obvious as to not be worth mentioning. But astonishingly, many people skip this step. Instead, they begin to assemble their portfolios by taking a trip to Wall Street's giant supermarket of financial products. These include mutual funds, exchange-traded funds (ETFs), annuities, insurance, trading systems, derivatives, or what have you. There's no shortage of things to buy. Nevertheless, this trip is a mistake. It's an extremely easy mistake to make because the financial services industry is forever engineering and promoting products to sell to investors. That's their job. If you read the business section of a newspaper, watch CNBC, read *Money* magazine, or log on to **TheStreet.com,** you'll notice that these media outlets are all supported by advertising. They're full of ads for products that, without quite coming out and saying so, seem like they're going to make you a lot of money.

A person with an interest in investing who turns on the TV or opens the newspaper is very quickly going to be funneled into the financial-products showroom and dazzled with the features and benefits of this brokerage or that five-star mutual fund or some other financial solution to his life's problem. Like a fish swimming into a trap, the innocent rube won't see the walls closing in. Pretty soon he's wondering which commodities fund has the best three-year track record, when he should be asking: *What am I doing here?*

By analogy, this is like solving your transportation problem by first visiting the Corvette showroom. Now, undeniably, Corvettes are beautiful to behold and wondrous to drive. It's exciting to salivate over the brochure, discerning if the LeMans Blue or Monterey Red Metallic would look better in your driveway and wondering whether the seven-speaker Bose sound system is an essential extra-cost option. These are fun fantasies, but this is the wrong place to start.

In the case of our personal finances, gaping questions open like a chasm in front of us. We stare into the abyss, and the abyss stares back into us, right down to our toes. No wonder we'd rather go shopping.

Assets and Liabilities

Our friend investment guru Ray Lucia says something very smart: Life is about matching assets with liabilities.

We have many kinds of both. In the asset column, there are the savings we've accumulated. We have the equity in our homes, if we own our homes. We have our health, education, and career, as well as our connections, good looks, and dazzling social skills. We might have an inheritance coming or have nine sons in a row who can play baseball. If we marry, we may hitch our caboose to the financial star of our partner. We all have the incalculable blessing of living in the United States: a free country with open markets that allows us to profit to the extent of our abilities, both with our labor and with our capital (our investments). This was a historically unheard-of opportunity until the United States came along, and it's our legacy from earlier generations of Americans who suffered in countless ways to present it to us on a silver platter.

As for liabilities, there are all too many. The Godzilla of personal liabilities is the task of largely self-funding our own retirements. This chore all by itself is so daunting that unless we're already rich, it will require virtually every spare dollar we can throw at it. There are plenty more worries, too: paying for a house, private school for our children, a wedding for ourselves or our daughters, a private nursing home for our in-laws, and any number of medical procedures that aren't covered by Medicare (an increasingly long list in the future). We might want to take a trip around the world, join a country club, or buy a boat or a vacation home—to say nothing of the everyday living expenses that always add up to far more than we expect; and the unrelenting, pitiless tax bills that periodically clean out our bank accounts along the way.

If you haven't already done so, there's no time like the present to consider the lifetime liabilities you'll face, as well as the lifetime assets you'll be able to bring to bear upon them. Conveniently, your authors have written a book on this very topic *(Yes, You Can Get a Financial Life!)* that will help you get started.

The Near and the Far

If we lay out our financial obligations on a timeline, we discover that our liabilities fall into three categories: *short-term, intermediate-term,* and *long-term.*

- *Short-term liabilities* are those that we will have to meet over the next few years.

- *Intermediate-term liabilities* are those that we will incur over, let's say, the next four to nine years.

- *Long-term liabilities* are those that lie ten years out and beyond.

The time frame is important because it determines how much risk we can take with the assets we put against them, which in turn puts a ceiling on the returns we might realistically expect.

- Short-term liabilities = very low risk/return assets

- Intermediate-term liabilities = intermediate risk/return assets

- Long-term liabilities = higher risk/return assets

We can't afford to take much risk when it comes to paying the mortgage next month—the money had better be there or we're out on the sidewalk. But we can afford to take a fair piece of risk with our 401(k) plan, earmarked for our retirement 20 years from now. If it loses money in the short run, we have time to play catch-up.

There will be lots more on this later. For now, the important point to keep in mind is that we aren't investing for its own sake; we're always investing toward some goal. This means that the investments we make should fit with our near- and far-term financial plans. We want one set of investments to pay Junior's tuition check next fall, another set for the down payment on the second home in Maine we've always dreamed of, and a third group of investments to cover our retirement in the far-flung but inevitable future.

Here's something interesting: Our short-term goals tend to be non-negotiable. We don't want the leasing company to repossess our cars, and we can't have our Visa card denied at the grocery store. Without short-term liquidity, our lives screech to a halt. For that reason, our short-term money should be kept in something safe and liquid, such as a high-yielding money market fund.

Our intermediate-term goals are often items over which we have some discretion. How much do we really want to spend on that house, that boat, that bar mitzvah, or that wedding? If we can't afford Skidmore, maybe little Suzie can go to State. If we're fortunate enough to have capital left over after we've met our short- and long-term liabilities, these intermediate-term goals might best be funded with a low-expense, balanced mutual fund that holds a roughly equal mix of cash, stocks, and bonds. You can easily find one at Vanguard or Fidelity.

Our long-term goals may seem far away, but they're also non-negotiable, even if we pretend otherwise. Very few Baby Boomers and Gen Xers are going to reach retirement and say, "What a dope I was to save all this money! How will I ever spend it?" No, they live in deep denial, and one day the cupboard will be bare. It is essential to plan for and fund these long-term obligations. Most of this book will be about how to do so, since this is where most of the problem lies.

For example, you want to be able to put together scenarios like this one: Imagine that you're 35 years old with $35,000 saved up in a 401(k) for retirement. If you continue to save $6,000 a year in a portfolio that's 60 percent stocks and 40 percent bonds, you can retire at age 66 and confidently expect to pull $50,000 of today's dollars out annually thereafter, with only a 10 percent chance of running out of money by the age of 100.

This is replacing pure guesses with rational estimates. You'll want to insert the numbers that make sense in order to create the action plan you need. This book will specifically help you maximize the work done by the portfolio allocation you select, to help you get to your destination as painlessly as possible.

You, Baby—Nobody but You

When you start your quest to invest that first surplus dollar by visiting the giant financial-products showroom instead of taking a fearless inventory of your financial future, you set yourself up to be fitted with the wrong solutions. Wall Street is in the completely justifiable business of making money for itself, and it has an enormous budget to market its services. But in so doing, it risks superimposing its own products over your personal situations, regardless of the fit. Just as the Corvette salesman will be more concerned with selling the Corvette than with determining whether the Corvette is really the right car for you, so too will the financial-services salesman ultimately be more concerned with his income than with yours. This is human nature. The task is to match Wall Street's marketing muscle with your own consumer savvy and assertiveness. You do this by first focusing on your own needs, developing a plan and an asset allocation, and only then selectively choosing investments to fund it.

In other words, as Warren Buffett says, don't ask the barber if you need a haircut. Step 1 is to look in the mirror and determine for yourself what you need. Then you can allocate scarce capital appropriately, matching your investments to your liabilities. Portfolio management doesn't begin with a selection of juicy five-star investments—it starts with *you*.

Chapter Two

Step 2: It's Your Whole Portfolio That Matters

Sentimental fools that we are, your authors are nostalgic for life in the United States during the 1950s. In 1951, color television was introduced. Remington Rand Corporation developed the first electronic digital Universal Automatic Computer, UNIVAC. Ben Hogan won the U.S. Open, while the New York Yankees beat the New York Giants 4–2 in the World Series. Best Picture that year was *An American in Paris,* while Humphrey Bogart took the Best Actor Oscar for *The African Queen.* On Broadway, *Guys and Dolls* won the Tony for Best Musical. The two most popular novels that year were *From Here to Eternity* and *The Caine Mutiny.* Meanwhile, on TV, Lucille Ball, Jack Benny, Ernie Kovacs, Groucho Marx, and Red Skelton were creating a golden age of television comedy. On radio and records, Perry Como, Nat King Cole, Tony Bennett, and Rosemary Clooney topped the Hit Parade.

Back in 1951, when people wanted to invest their surplus capital beyond a passbook savings account or buying a U.S. Savings Bond, they typically did so through the intermediary of a stockbroker. He might suggest that U.S. Steel looked like a good bet, and if his clients liked his pitch they might spring for 100 shares. Since the brokerage firms all engaged in price-fixing, commissions were ridiculously high by today's standards. Incredibly, they were in the range of 2 percent of the entire transaction, with a minimum of a certain amount.

The strategy was to pick winning stocks. By taking care to analyze each individual holding, a person could accumulate a number of hot positions. Since the postwar American economy was booming, most portfolios containing the name-brand issues of the day performed well. The operative philosophy of the era was summed up by Gerald Loeb, in his 1935 classic *The Battle for Investment Survival*: ". . . once you attain competency, diversification is undesirable. One or two, or at most three or four, securities should be bought. . . ." And in the concluding Postscript section of that book, he wrote: "My feeling is that competent investors will never be satisfied beating the averages as it were, by a few small percentage points . . ." This was standard thinking.

Meanwhile, at the University of Chicago, graduate student Harry Markowitz was bothered by this line of reasoning. After all, if returns were all that mattered, then it would make perfect sense to have a portfolio consisting of just one stock: the one with the fastest-growing dividends that would ultimately determine the stock's value. You might even hold several stocks within a given industry, if all the prospects for all of them appeared equally bright. But Markowitz knew that smart investors didn't do this. Owning a single stock, or even several stocks from within the same industry, could turn out to be very risky. What if the analysts were wrong? What if the future proved to be different from what was expected? Investing wasn't a one-variable problem that centered exclusively on expected returns.

Like boxers, real-world investors might have jabbed with one hand, but they kept the other hand close to guard their chin. They tempered their search for returns with the need to protect themselves from risk. Even if the risk/reward trade-off for a single stock appeared favorable, this advantage could be undone if an investor held several stocks with similar risks. The risks inherent in a portfolio of stocks depended on how all of the various securities acted in concert. Sophisticated investors *diversified* by holding multiple assets that behaved differently from one another. If U.S. Steel fluctuated with the fortunes of the economy, they might also own Consolidated Edison, an electrical utility that charged prices that were closely regulated by the government. The fortunes of these two companies would not be highly correlated. They might also invest in General Mills, which made Wheaties and Cheerios, since people would be eating breakfast in good times and bad. And maybe they'd buy an indestructible company like General Motors and take a flier on a hot technology stock such as Polaroid. Each of these companies would have its own ups and downs, but the point was that they wouldn't all be up and down at the same time in sync with each other. Some would zig while others zagged.

What did this mean for investors? It meant the returns they got would be the weighted average of all the returns of all the companies they owned. Their risks, though, would *not* be the weighted average of all the risks of each of the organizations—because sometimes one would be up when another was down, and vice versa. In other words, by choosing a diversified lot of businesses, the risks would cancel each other out to some extent. A properly diversified stock portfolio could deliver better returns for the same amount of risk.

Here was something else that was new: All this could be quantified mathematically. You could try to construct a portfolio with the highest expected return (but with the least amount of expected risk), or you could try to build a portfolio with the least amount of risk (but with the highest expected return). Or you could build one anywhere in between, along the path (the "efficient frontier," as it was called) that connected these two points. You couldn't know these numbers in advance with certainty, of course, but at least you had some basis for making a rational estimate: the historical risks and returns of the portfolio's constituent stocks. It was no longer purely a matter of luck or guesswork.

With this insight, the focus of investing shifted from individual security selection to how each one interacted with all the others. It wasn't solely about returns or risk, but about both at the same time: getting the optimal *risk-adjusted returns*. Portfolios were judged based on how *efficient* they were at delivering them.

Markowitz wrote this up in an article for *The Journal of Finance* on "Portfolio Selection" in 1952, and received the Sveriges Riksbank Prize in Economic Sciences in Memory of Alfred Nobel (better known as the Nobel Prize) in 1990 for his seminal insight, which had given birth to Modern Portfolio Theory.

Strangely, the earth didn't move upon publication of this article. Investors kept on trading much as before, uninfluenced by the Markowitz and the pointy-headed thinkers in Hyde Park, home of the University of Chicago.

Even more strangely, for many individual investors right up to the present, the universe still hasn't moved. The talk around the locker room is still about the latest hot stock. Some guy is always bragging about how he made a killing in Google (which means he bought ten shares).

Let's revisit Ben's and Tad's portfolios, with an eye to this question: Which one is more diversified, and thus likely to deliver a bigger return for the amount of risk assumed? Or, looking at it from the other end, which portfolio is more concentrated, so that its holdings are likely to rise and fall as one?

Ben's List

- Templeton Emerging Markets Income Fund, Inc.: numerous bonds from many countries

- Cohen & Steers Realty Majors: numerous real estate investment trusts

- Standard & Poor's Depository Receipts: 500 companies

- Diamonds Trust: 30 companies

- Boeing Co.: one company, aerospace

Tad's List

- Playboy Enterprises, Inc. (PLA): one company, leisure and entertainment

- Krispy Kreme Doughnut Corp. (KKD): one company, food and beverage

- Harley-Davidson, Inc. (HOG): one company, leisure and entertainment

- Anheuser-Busch Companies, Inc. (BUD): one company, food and beverage

- TiVo, Inc. (TIVO): one company, leisure and entertainment

Right away, you can see that Ben owns close to a thousand different securities: foreign bonds, real estate investment trusts, and stocks. His risks are highly diversified across sectors. Tad, on the other hand, holds only five companies. Furthermore, these organizations all hang by a single thread: hedonism. His risks are extremely focused, and had hedonism come especially into favor during this period, his returns might have been enormous. Ben didn't take anything like the risks that Tad did, and so, like the tortoise, he won the race.

What about the argument that Tad is cleverly betting on a reliable strain of human behavior? Isn't his penetrating psychological insight that people are pleasure-seeking worth something?

Yes and no. Human beings do tend to be self-indulgent, this is true. The problem is that this isn't a new or unique observation. It's a well-known feature of human nature. As such, *it was already built into the price of the stocks when Tad bought them.* In 1953 (the year after Modern Portfolio Theory was discovered), when Hugh Hefner began publishing and *Playboy* was very much an unproven proposition, it would have been a great investment to loan Hef a couple of thousand dollars to help him get it launched. But by 2003, this enterprise was 50 years old. For Tad's portfolio to have been especially successful, there would have to have been some fresh news. Men's desire to look at pictures of naked women, drink beer, watch TV, eat doughnuts, or ride Harleys would have to be inordinately greater than it was before. Absent some compelling new factor, the ordinary level of people's desire to do these things was already built into the price of the stocks.

Well, you might say, that's just Tad. Not the brightest crayon in the box, as far as investing is concerned. Gentle reader, dare we remind you of the Internet/telecom boom of only a few years back? How many people had portfolios that looked like this?

Typical Internet/Telecom-Era Portfolio

- CMGI

- Global Crossing

- Yahoo!

- AOL

- JDS Uniphase

- Qualcomm

- Cisco

- Lucent

- DoubleClick

- Fidelity Select Electronics

- Firsthand Technology Value

These names read like a bad acid flashback. Everyone had portfolios chock full of these stocks and their bastard spawn. They delivered astronomical returns—for a while. Then every shoe-shine boy got into the act, convinced that they were masters of the universe just because they bought stocks that were soaring upward. As Warren Buffett observed, investors were dancing at a ball where the clock had no hands. When midnight tolled, everything turned into pumpkins and mice. Folks lost 80 percent of their portfolios' value (except for many who went "on margin"—borrowing against the value of their securities to buy even more of the same—and lost everything). People's retirement dreams drove right off a cliff. Why? Because *they were unfamiliar with the basic tenets of portfolio construction that had been worked out almost half a century earlier.* Instead of diversifying risk, they invested in ways that concentrated it, with disastrous results. By comparison, Tad's hapless portfolio is a model of probity and restraint.

When we said that the world went right on investing the old-fashioned way in spite of the advances in financial theory, we forgot to mention one group who took the findings seriously. These were some of the institutional investors.

When we buy and sell stocks (unlike, for instance, bets in a game of poker), the transactions are anonymous. We don't get to see who's on the other side of the table. Most of the trading today is done by hedge funds, pension plans, endowments, and other large institutional investors. Even their most junior people have M.B.A.s in finance from prestigious universities and earn six-figure salaries the first year out of school. They're hyperaware of the potential risks and rewards of their trades. When we buy or sell 100 shares of some stock we heard about on CNBC's *Power Lunch,* they're just as likely as not to be taking the other side. Would you feel differently about making the trade if you knew that a team of gunslingers from Goldman Sachs was betting against you? We certainly would.

How can we protect ourselves? If Step 1 was to understand our individual goals and needs, Step 2 is to stop investing the way people did back when Patti Page's "(How Much Is That) Doggie in the Window?" was topping the charts. It's time we moved our investing into the rock 'n' roll era.

The GLOM Portfolio

If we were to be ruthlessly honest with ourselves, many of us would probably have to admit that there was no one overarching and cogent investment philosophy behind our various holdings. Instead, we have *agglomerative* portfolios—what we'll call GLOM portfolios, for short.

Here's the story of the typical GLOM investor: He started investing ten years ago when his parents told him to open an IRA, and he put $2,000 into one. It's still sitting in the money market account. He keeps getting the statements in the mail but isn't quite sure what to do. Then he joined a company and checked some box that put 3 percent of his salary into a 401(k). It's invested half in company stock and half in two mutual funds that have important-sounding names. One of them is "Growth" something, he thinks. Then during the "New Paradigm" era he opened an account at E*trade and invested in that list of stocks above. He put $20,000 in it, and at one point it was worth more than $50,000. Now it's worth about $14,000. He meant to sell, but these stocks have to come back up—don't they? Finally, his brother-in-law became a stockbroker and went to work for a well-known brokerage firm. So our GLOM investor gave his relative his bonus last year and ended up with an annuity and a half-dozen individual stocks. They don't seem to be going up as much as the market is, though.

Or else there's some similar story. Most people don't invest all at once, informed by the latest research in financial theory. They wander through the Wall Street supermarket, picking up whatever scraps are dangled in front of them at the time. The result is the GLOM portfolio, and our description possibly matches your experience to some degree.

What does it add up to—not just in total dollars, but in overall expected risks and returns? What would it look like on a pie chart? You probably don't know. It's going to take you *somewhere* (The poorhouse? The cleaners?), but is it going to take you where you want to go? Is it going to send Missy to grad school? Is it going to pay for that home overlooking the 17th hole at Pebble Beach after you retire?

We fear that for many people, the GLOM portfolio will be a disaster. It's not that you don't want to know what you have and what it means, but you don't have the tools to pull it all together. No one taught you finance in high school. No one told you that—in addition to working your day job—you were going to have to become a financial planner. You're going to have to play catch-up.

We're going to help you move from a GLOM portfolio to a more thoughtfully considered asset allocation. It means you have to diversify your investments to a point where you're getting an efficient trade-off between expected returns and the risks it takes to get them.

We'll take a closer look at these risks in the next chapter.

Chapter Three

Step 3: Take on Risk Intelligently

People are forever bragging about their investment returns. Never mind all the cases where they're conveniently forgetting to mention all their losses, are just plain wrong, or are outright lying. This talk is meaningless unless you know how much risk they took to get the returns they brag about. The guy at the next locker whose portfolio was up 15 percent last year while yours was only up 7 percent? He may not know it, but for the chances he was taking, he should have been up 30 percent. Knowing returns without understanding risks is like knowing only one team's score in a football game.

If it were simple to take a very small amount of risk and capture a big reward, everyone would do it and we would all be rich. Sadly, this just doesn't happen. Figure 3.1 on the next page shows why.

Figure 3.1: Risks & Returns of Asset Classes 1988–2006

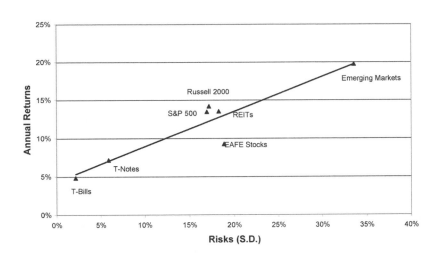

Figure 3.1 shows the risks and returns of various asset classes over the past 18 years. Risk here is defined as *standard deviation,* a concept we'll get to shortly. For now it's enough to know that it measures how widely the returns fluctuate up and down. At the one extreme, we have T-Bills in the lower left-hand corner, offering low returns for low risks. At the other end of the line, we have emerging market stocks, offering high returns but for high risks. The only slight outlier is the MSCI EAFE Index of stocks from Europe, Australia, and the Far East. Its returns were suppressed over this period by the collapse of Japan's Nikkei stock market in the early 1990s—the index's biggest single component.

The big idea here is: If you want rewards, you have to take risks. If you don't want to take risks, you can't expect too much in the way of reward. This explains investment returns as well as why your palms sweat before you ask the prettiest girl in your class to the prom. (*Author's note:* She accepted! Thank you, Polly.)

Since expected risks are rarely disclosed, how can investors be expected to make informed choices about their use of capital? Being told that "investments may lose value" is like being told that "explosives can be dangerous." Are we talking about a firecracker or an atom bomb? Without any knowledge of the trade-offs between expected risks and expected rewards for specific investments and combinations of these investments, it's difficult to participate in the markets intelligently. No wonder so many people leave their 401(k) assets languishing in cash.

As an investor under capitalism, we might go so far as to say that you're being paid by the markets precisely to assume risk. The only "riskless" investment is cash in an FDIC-insured savings account. Money kept there usually earns a very small negative return after inflation. In Jeremy Siegel's classic *Stocks for the Long Run,* there's a famous chart showing how one dollar invested in cash in 1802 was worth seven cents by 2001. Even an extremely patient and long-lived investor wasn't rewarded for following this seemingly safe strategy.

Taking a step up on the risk ladder, you might lend money to the government by buying a government bond. Here the risk is very small, and the returns to bond holders have also been proportionately circumscribed over time. One dollar invested in government bonds in 1802 would have been worth $952 in 2001, according to Professor Siegel.

For most investors, though, taking risk in pursuit of reward means investing in the stock market. Here the risks are substantial—you can lose a lot of money in a downturn. In 1987, investors lost 23 percent of their money in a single day, and no one saw it coming. Nevertheless, the long-term rewards are tremendous. Siegel's chart shows how a dollar invested in the U.S. stock market in 1802 would have been worth $599,605 on a total returns basis by 2001—even after all the wars, recessions, depressions, market panics, and so on along the way.

This is the kind of eye-popping return that investors are hoping for when they lay their money on the green felt table of the stock market. They are glamorized by the lovely lady, "Rita Returns," but overlook her hideous sister, "Rayette Risk," who accompanies her wherever she goes.

This mistake is all too easy to make, for the simple reason that performance is visible, while risk is mostly invisible—usually until it's too late. When we open *The Wall Street Journal* and tune in to CNBC, they tell us how much the market is up or down. They don't tell us how risky it is. Those monthly brokerage statements may state our returns (if we're lucky), but they're mute on the subject of the chances we took to earn them. This is true in spite of the fact that the scary part is as readily quantifiable as the good part.

Taking on excess risk is what led to the horrible losses when the tech bubble burst, and indeed, when every bubble bursts, as bubbles do. We always assume that we can stand near the exits and unload our overpriced stock to some greater fool who's on his way into the tent. We think we'll be the exception to the general rule, but then it turns out that we are the greater fools. This happens so often that it could be a country-and-western song.

The prudent investor is always aware of how much risk he's taking and tries to position his investments somewhere along the path (technically known as the "efficient frontier") that represents the best trade-off between risk and return. This sounds complicated, and while perfection is impossible, in practice an ordinary investor can do it pretty well.

Consider this: The entire stock market has a certain historical level of risk, as well as a corresponding level of return. Since it contains every stock, it's extremely diversified. This means that the returns we get for owning the entire stock market incorporate a tremendous amount of the diversification benefit that Markowitz was extolling.

When we own the whole stock market, we're getting paid a market-wide rate of return for assuming a market-wide level of risk. On the other hand, when we own 12 randomly selected stocks, what we typically find is that their returns will converge toward those of the stock market as a whole, but their volatility will be greater. This means that we're suffering too much risk for the returns we're getting because we could always get rid of this unnecessary extra risk just by supersizing. We can easily do this through the simple expedient of purchasing a low-expense stock market index fund. There's no shortage of broad stock market indexes (such as the Russell 3000, the Dow Jones Total Market, the S&P 500, and the Wilshire 5000) and index mutual funds that track them.

There are several other wondrous features of owning the entire stock market. Not only are we highly diversified, but the market as a whole does an excellent job of pricing the stocks within it. Remember how Tad thought that his hedonism theme would outperform? That was naïve—it had been priced into his stocks long before he bought them. It may have been news to Tad, but as far as the stock market was concerned, it was yesterday's papers.

This isn't to say that the meeting of buyers and sellers results in every stock being perfectly priced with a perfectly balanced weighting of all its future prospects and liabilities. But it is true that such mispricings as do occur tend to be both (a) random (that is, stocks are just as likely to be priced too high as too low) and (b) quickly corrected when discovered. This is called the *efficient market theory:* the notion that the actions of buyers and sellers in markets speedily incorporate all available information into stock prices. Most of the arguments today aren't about whether the broad strokes of the theory are correct (they are), but are concerned with determining exactly how efficient the market is, where the inefficiencies may lie, and how and whether such flaws might be profitably exploited.

If you find a list of the top-ten mutual fund managers for the past ten years and then put your money into these ten funds, what you'll likely discover in a decade is that they weren't the next ten years' top performers. Instead, the record of the this group of market gurus will "regress to the mean," which means that it will fall from its current high level. You'll buy at the top and ride their roller coaster down. This is counterintuitive, but is exactly what happens, as demonstrated in study after study (see, for example, Yan Wang's paper on "Money Fund Flows, Performance Persistence, and Manager Skill" from the Financial Management Association's 2006 Annual Meeting). The performance of the market index mutual funds, meanwhile, will be . . . right at the index, less the very slight management fees.

Fidelity Investments will sell you shares in its Spartan Total Stock Market Index Fund (ticker: FSTMX) at a charge of 1/10th of a percent of your holdings per year. Stockbrokers, investment advisors, and actively managed mutual funds can charge 10 or 15 times this amount for routinely delivering inferior performance. The bitter truth is that simple index funds outperform most of their actively managed peers. Not every year, to be sure, but often enough that most investors will be way ahead of the game choosing this strategy as their baseline approach over their investment lifetime.

As John Bogle pointed out in the *Financial Analysts Journal* for November/December 2005, after expenses, taxes, and inflation, the average actively managed mutual fund delivered only 34 percent of the profit of an S&P 500 Index fund from 1983 to 2003. *Indeed, shifting from the GLOM portfolio to buying and holding a few broad market index funds is perhaps the most important move ordinary investors can make to supercharge their portfolios.* It will put them ahead of most of the active managers both because it's so much cheaper, and because index funds are so efficient at delivering a high ratio of return for the extremely diversified, market-wide risks they're taking.

What about picking hot stocks? Nobel laureate William Sharpe's Capital Asset Pricing Model suggests that getting a higher-than-market rate of return on your equity investments entails buying riskier stocks, so there's no free lunch in this pursuit. Big returns mean big risks. What about market timing? As early as 1975, Sharpe had also written a dispositive paper for the *Financial Analysts Journal* on the "Likely Gains from Market Timing" that concluded that managers should "probably avoid market timing altogether." The retail public comprise the worst market timers of all, since they're forever inundating the latest hot funds with so many fresh dollars that whatever returns these funds once delivered are immediately neutralized by an ocean of cash. This is why Bogle found (in the same paper just cited) that retail investors in the average actively managed mutual funds—after accounting for their bad in-and-out timing decisions as well as fund expenses—secured only 24 percent of the profits of the simple buy-and-hold investor in an S&P index fund. For most investors, the quest to beat the market will be like mounting an expedition to find the abominable snowman: potentially profitable, but more likely to end in costly disappointment.

Risky Business

Risk is usually defined as *volatility:* how much your portfolio jumps up and down over a given time period. The statistical way of measuring this (fasten your seat belt—this is one of the very few mathematical concepts you need to be familiar with) is your portfolio's *standard deviation.* That tells you how likely it is that your portfolio's performance will be up or down a certain amount from its expected average performance. You need to know the standard deviation of your portfolio the way a doctor needs to know your heart rate. As we've seen, discussions of investing are meaningless unless we know the risks incurred. People prattle endlessly about their returns but never mention the chances they took to get them because they have no idea what they are. Serious investors can't afford this level of ignorance.

Let's put some numbers to the face of risk. Since the end of World War II, the S&P 500 Index has had an average annual return (dividends plus capital appreciation) of roughly 13 percent. Over this same long historical period, it has had a average annual standard deviation of roughly 17 percent. What does this mean? In any given year, there is about a two-thirds chance that the total returns of the S&P 500 Index are going to fall within one standard deviation (plus or minus 17 percentage points) of its mean total (13 percent). That would range somewhere between a high annual return of 30 percent (the 13 percent mean plus the 17 percent standard deviation) to a low annual return of minus 4 percent (the 13 percent mean minus the 17 percent standard deviation).

In any given year, there is about a 95 percent chance that the returns will fall within *two* standard deviations of the mean, or somewhere between 47 percent (the 13 percent mean plus two times the 17 percent standard deviation) on the upside and minus 21 percent (the 13 percent mean minus two times the 17 percent standard deviation) on the downside. In other words, in an ordinary bad year you might lose 4 percent of your money investing in the S&P 500 Index, and in a really bad year you might lose 21 percent or more. This gives you a palpable feel for the risk you are taking.

The calculations are far from exact, but they're as close to a crystal ball as we are likely to get. What's more important, they provide us with a yardstick that allows us to compare the risks of different investment strategies.

It makes no sense to supercharge our portfolios by piling on high-performance assets unless we know how much risk we're taking on in the process. The point isn't to go for broke; it's to avoid going broke by making our portfolios as efficient as they can be, given the overall level of risk that makes sense for our personal situations.

Reducing Risk

What if 17 percent is still too high a standard deviation for our taste? What if you can't stomach the likelihood of losing 21 percent of your money in a bad year? Wise is the person who has this degree of self-knowledge. The time to decide you've taken on too much risk isn't the day after the market is down 20 percent. If you wait until then and sell when your stocks are beaten down, it will prove to be a very expensive shellacking. Nevertheless, this is one of the most common mistakes investors make.

It's all very well to know that standard deviation is a way to measure a portfolio's risk, but where can you find this vital piece of information? You'll study your brokerage statements in vain for it.

One way is to log on to Morningstar (**www.morningstar.com**). Go to the "Portfolio" tab and enter the tickers of the individual holdings in your portfolio as well as how many shares you own of each. Then, you could customize your portfolio view to include the "three-year return" and "standard deviation" measurement. Voilà! It shows these measurements for the past three years—at least, for each investment considered individually, if not for the portfolio taken as a whole. As wonderful as the Morningstar site is, however, we think there's even a better way, which we'll get to shortly.

How can you tame the risk level of your portfolio—that is, lower its standard deviation—to a degree you can live with? This question was answered by Nobelist James Tobin in February 1958 ("Liquidity Preference as Behavior Towards Risk" in *The Review of Economic Studies*).

The way to change the volatility of your portfolio is by borrowing or lending money against it. If you want to increase the volatility of your portfolio, the solution is to borrow against it (go "on margin"). During the Internet/telecom bubble, many people were making so much money so effortlessly that they decided to borrow from their brokers to buy even more of the same stocks that were making them so rich. A $100 investment could control $150 in the stock market through this simple strategy. Paying a few measly percentage points in interest was nothing when a tech portfolio was racing up 60 percent every year. This was truly a magical way to get rich.

The downside came when the bubble burst. Then the leverage operated in reverse, and instead of losing 75 percent of their money alongside the NASDAQ, people were completely wiped out. The risks of owning volatile stocks were compounded because they were all from the same sector (which means that they didn't diversify each other), and then they got put on steroids when bought with borrowed money. There are few more chilling events than getting a margin call—that is, a call from your broker when the price of the securities you're holding as collateral has fallen, demanding that you deposit more money so your account can be brought up to a minimum balance because you don't have enough value remaining in your stocks to cover the margin requirements.

The same principle that led these investors to ruin can save all of us. Instead of borrowing more money to invest, we can lend money. That is to say, we can buy bonds. Figure 3.1 showed how bonds are the "Steady Eddies" of the investment world, having low risk and low return. The beauty of them is that they don't just have a low correlation with the stock market, they usually have a small but *negative* correlation. When stocks are down, bonds might even be up. This can smooth out our rides considerably. To the extent that we want to dampen the volatility of our stock portfolios, we just add bonds.

Now, there are many types of bonds. There are bonds of all different maturities and credit qualities. As far as capital-appreciation portfolios are concerned, we're only talking about short-maturity, high quality bonds. We're emphatically *not* talking about long-term bonds or junk bonds.

Table 3.1 shows how adding different quantities of these bonds to a stock portfolio (the S&P 500 Index) affects its potential for rewards and risks.

Table 3.1: Rewards and Risks of Stock + Bond Portfolios 1977–2006						
% Stocks	**0%**	**20%**	**40%**	**60%**	**80%**	**100%**
% Bonds	**100%**	**80%**	**60%**	**40%**	**20%**	**0%**
Average Total Returns	7.5%	8.9%	10.2%	11.5%	12.8%	14.2%
Standard Deviation	4.3%	5.5%	8.3%	11.5%	15.0%	18.5%
Really Bad Year	-1%	-2%	-6%	-12%	-17%	-23%

Remember that these numbers aren't carved in stone—they reflect holding various mixtures of the S&P 500 with short-term (one to three year maturity) government bonds, and show their annual returns and standard deviations from 1977 through 2006. They're illustrative. As the percentage of bonds in the portfolio goes from 0 percent to 100 percent (from right to left in Table 3.1), the total returns we might see in a really bad year improve from minus 23 percent to minus 1 percent. This is the stabilizing power that bonds bring to a portfolio.

Of course, our upside returns are compromised to the same degree; but for right now, we're just focusing on limiting our downside risk. Another extremely interesting feature of adding bonds to a portfolio is that the amount of improvement we get in volatility doesn't improve exactly in a straight line. Figure 3.2 plots the same data as Table 3.1, but with the annual returns on the vertical axis and the standard deviation/risks on the horizontal axis. Each triangle represents one of the portfolios above, ranging from the all-bond portfolio at the lower left (low returns, low risk) to the all-stock portfolio at the upper right (high returns, high risk).

Figure 3.2: Risks & Returns of Stock + Bond Portfolios

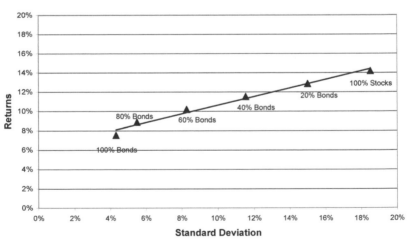

Notice how, on the far right, adding the first dollop of bonds (moving from 100 percent stocks to 80 percent stocks and 20 percent bonds) takes us a long way toward reducing risk (standard deviation, on the horizontal axis) with a fairly modest drop in returns (the vertical axis). On the other hand, going the last mile (moving from 80 percent bonds to 100 percent bonds) on the far left causes a big falloff in returns in exchange for only a modest drop in risk. The "sweet spot" of the return/risk trade-off for this portfolio is somewhere between 20 percent and 80 percent bonds.

An all-stock or an all-bond portfolio isn't usually as efficient as one that contains both asset classes. The right mixture for you will vary with your goals. The basic principle to keep in mind is to optimize the stock side of your portfolio first, and then tamp it down with bonds to whatever extent is necessary or desirable to control for risk.

What specific bonds should you use? As with stocks, we recommend a simple low-expense index fund, in this case using short-term, high-quality bonds. Table 3.2 lists some good examples.

Table 3.2: Bond Funds to Control Portfolio Volatility

Fund	Ticker	Duration	Credit	Expense Ratio
Vanguard Short-Term Bond Index	VBISX	2.4 Years	AA	0.18
Fidelity Short-Term Bond	FSHBX	1.7 Years	AA	0.44
For Taxable Accounts:				
Vanguard Limited-Term Tax-Exempt	VMLTX	2.6 Years	AA	0.16
Fidelity Short-Intermediate Muni Income	FSTFX	2.8 Years	AA	0.41

Love Hurts, and So Does Volatility

Let's say we're 65 today, with a million-dollar portfolio invested 60 percent into the S&P 500 Index and 40 percent into the Lehman Bond Aggregate (an index that's often used as a proxy for the total U.S. bond market). If we assume that our portfolio will earn the flat historical return going forward (a little more than 10 percent), then we can pull out $85,000 a year and not run out of money until we turn 90. This leads us to plan one type of retirement.

What happens when we bring risk into the picture? With a portfolio that fluctuates in value as much as a 60/40 stock/bond allocation usually does, even if it still earns the usual 10 percent on average, we can't pull out nearly as much. If we try to pull $85,000 a year out of our million-dollar nest egg, we discover that half of those possible future scenarios have us going bust by the time we reach age 83. If we want to play it reasonably safe (a 10 percent chance of running out of money by the time we hit 90), we can only pull out $53,000 a year, not $85,000. This leads us to plan a very different sort of retirement. In the first instance, looking only at the long-term 10 percent annual return from the stock market, we were (wrongly) assuming that we were getting our payout risk free. If only!

Volatility isn't just bad because it leads to a panic attack when we open our statements and see our stocks are down. It costs us money by cutting our long-term returns, as well as the distribution that we may safely take from those returns.

The Risk That Matters Most

Ultimately, however, the risks of your portfolio can't be boiled down to its standard deviation. The real risk is that your portfolio fails to meet your investment goals (Step 1). It's possible that a portfolio that's very low risk in terms of volatility and that has you sleeping comfortably at night should really be keeping you wide awake because it has a very high risk of underfunding your retirement. In the end, the risks that really matter are the risks of not meeting your financial objectives. By comparison, standard deviation is only a measure of the bumpiness of the ride along the way. Standard deviation is much fussed over by finance types because it's readily quantifiable, but in comparison it's small potatoes.

The securities industry and the government bodies that regulate it have this backwards. They think that what matters is an inner psychological state called your "risk tolerance." The idea here is that if you're a riverboat gambler type of person, then it's fine to trade in risky options, but if you're a spinster librarian with three kittens, then you'd better stick to CDs and annuities. This is like a doctor saying that your psychological preference to wear or not wear a cast should be a factor in evaluating how to treat your broken leg. *In fact, your psychological predisposition to take or shun risk has nothing to do with how you should invest.* You should pursue the method that's most likely to achieve your investment goals, period, full stop. If that means having to watch your portfolio lose money along the way, then so be it. That's precisely what you're getting paid to do. The entire concept of "risk tolerance" should be discarded and replaced with your "running out of money" tolerance.

If you ever opened a brokerage account, you were probably asked about how much risk you can take. This is a stupid question, because how can you be expected to know? Even if you're told that the S&P 500 index has a standard deviation of 15 percent, what does this really mean to you, experientially? Unless you're a statistician and a long-term investor who has been through some big gulps in the market, it probably signifies nothing. In practice, the only real meaning to the standard deviation is that if you're likely to panic and sell when a big drop hits, that's bad. Many investors fall into this category, which is why their returns fall so far short of what they could have been if they'd stayed the course.

Instead, they're forever buying high in a state of confidence and selling low in despair, perfectly mistiming the market. They don't believe that—over the long run—their investment returns will revert to the long-term expected mean.

One reason it's difficult for you to assess "risk tolerance" accurately has to do with the fact that losses and gains are psychologically asymmetrical: Losses hurt you more than gains feel good. There's also something called an "availability bias" built into your perception of risk. The 10 percent your portfolio is down this month is visible today—it jumps right out from your brokerage statement and grabs you by the collar. But the future when you're broke at the age of 85 because you didn't invest aggressively enough is invisible: It might as well occur in some galaxy far, far away.

Even if you knew yourself well enough to describe your risk tolerance perfectly, the answer is still irrelevant to what you *should* do. You should invest to meet your goals (like funding retirement), and then hang on through thick and thin. If you're a sensitive soul who can brook no paper losses, the solution is to get a grip, not to invest more "safely" if that means a likelihood of running out of money when you're old.

For most people with finite sums of money to invest in pursuit of ambitious long-term goals, this will involve putting 50 or 60 percent of their portfolios in the stock market, and probably more—even significantly more. To figure out how much risk *you* need to take to meet your financial goals, and to supercharge your portfolio to help you get there, you're going to need something called a Monte Carlo simulator.

Entering Monte Carlo

When the World War II physicists working on the atomic bomb at Los Alamos needed to calculate what might happen to the neutrons in the core of the nuclear reactor, they had to come up with a new mathematical approach to solve the problem because it couldn't be done with a pencil and paper. They ran large numbers of experiments using a computer to generate random numbers to account for the variability among the possible outcomes. Because the computer was in effect rolling dice, they called this technique "Monte Carlo" simulation, after the fashionable district in Monaco where the casinos are located. In recent decades, financial economists have adopted Monte Carlo simulations to model the uncertainties inherent in portfolio management. The computer revolution then put this capability on your desktop.

In William Bernstein's *The Intelligent Asset Allocator,* the good doctor experiments, putting together portfolios using a computer application called a "mean-variance optimizer." This earlier technology takes into account the historical means, standard deviations, and correlations among whatever investments are input, and solves the equation to calculate the perfect retroactive portfolio allocation for the time period entered. If the future were exactly like the past, this would be all we need. Unfortunately, the future is *not* just like the past, and Bernstein shows these custom-tailored portfolios have very poor predictive validity. Mean-variance optimization is a nifty teaching tool with little practical application. It overweights the hottest asset classes during the sampling period and then draws an arrow from them into the future. Remember the book *Dow 36,000?* In 1999, this bestseller's breathless title seemed within reach; but today, it's been demoted to a "New Paradigm" collectible. This illustrates the danger of making straight-line predictions into the future. (We don't mean to pick on *Dow 36,000.* It was just a meditation on market valuation with an oversexed title.)

The Monte Carlo simulator takes a different path toward making its projections. There are thousands of possible investment futures, but only one will happen. Instead of solving the equation to come up with the right backward-looking answer, Monte Carlo uses a computer's random number generator to construct sample sequences of future returns. After spawning thousands of possible scenarios for a given portfolio, the shape of its financial future begins to take form.

Monte Carlo tallies a "probability density function" that shows where the results cluster: which futures are more probable to occur, and which ones are statistical outliers. We can take the middle of the distribution (the median, or the 50th percentile case) as a reasonable assumption about where our investments might end up, as well as looking at high- and low-percentile cases (say, the 80th and 20th percentiles) to get an idea of the range of probable outcomes.

Most important, Monte Carlo simulation can put different portfolios through the same set of paces, letting us make head-to-head comparisons. What's more, it allows us to model cash flows in and out of a portfolio and calculate, for example, the probability of successfully funding our retirement. It's an effective tool to sharpen investment decisions.

This isn't a Ouija board, but it's as good an estimate as anyone can make right now. Monte Carlo takes a riddle wrapped in an enigma, and gives an answer like a red-hot chili pepper wrapped inside a hot tamale.

Making these kinds of calculations is the difference between planning a retirement and whistling in the dark. You can't do this at home using a yellow pad and a number two pencil, and you can't even do it if you're pretty good with Microsoft Excel. You need the specialized tools that finance professionals use.

Getting Monte Carlo

We like the Quantext Portfolio Planner (QPP) Monte Carlo simulator, available for a free fully functional trial download from **www.quantext.com**. QPP is the brainchild of former NASA scientist Geoff Considine, Ph.D., who has written extensively on the subject of Monte Carlo portfolio simulations. Dr. Considine keeps a library of valuable articles on the Quantext Website that we recommend as a follow-up to this book.

QPP easily allows users to vary key inputs such as their savings and withdrawal rates to determine the probability of successfully financing their retirements, and it has some other compelling features as well. For example, users can enter the individual tickers of their holdings, allowing the software to go online and collect the actual historical performance data. This is vital, because many early-generation Monte Carlo simulators just used generic long-term data for a few asset classes: stocks, bonds, commodities, and cash. None of us can supercharge our portfolios using such broad strokes. Also, because QPP uses specific tickers, the mutual fund or ETF data it collects already accounts for the exact impact of management fees on performance. It's not using cold index data that operates in some frictionless fairyland of no expenses.

Another important benefit of the QPP Monte Carlo simulator is that it doesn't automatically assume that recent history gives us the best window into the future. Rather, it posits that risk and reward are related (see Table 3.1 for a refresher), so if a security currently shows an unusually high level of return for the low amount of risk (or vice versa), it adjusts the risk and return projections to bring them in line with their long-term expected relationship. This middle-of-the-road approach can save us from making unrealistic projections when using fluky asset classes or sampling uncharacteristic time periods.

A Monte Carlo simulator is like a flight simulator for a portfolio. Not only can it help keep investors from crashing and burning, it can make them better pilots. It can help individuals take on the right amount of risk required to achieve their objectives, and to attain the return that's their due for the amount of risk they take. Yet unbelievably, apart from investment professionals and academics, very few people presently use Monte Carlo, even though it is the new standard in the field. Investors aren't using the one tool they really need in order to prepare for a future that will one day stare them in the face whether they've made adequate provisions for it or not.

Before speeding ahead, let's review what we've attempted to convey so far:

- Any set of investments only makes sense in relation to your investment goals.

- Most people pay great attention to picking a team of all-stars for their portfolios, but this effort is misdirected.

- Many people also pay enormous attention to performance, but overlook the risk it entails until it's too late because the risk is mostly invisible. Investors have to find it before it finds them.

- The tool used by sophisticated finance professionals today to discover and then control the risks and returns of their portfolios is the Monte Carlo simulator.

Chapter Four

Step 4: Diversify

Most investors pay lip service to the idea of a diversified portfolio, but what does this really mean? John Bogle, founder of the Vanguard Group and the patron saint of investors everywhere, very sensibly maintains that a broad index fund such as a total stock market index is the ideal equity holding. These funds contain thousands of securities, and so are massively diversified. At the other extreme, Charlie Munger, Warren Buffett's brilliant sidekick at Berkshire Hathaway, maintains that an investor can have a perfectly fine, well-diversified portfolio with ten stocks. Who's right?

As we'll see, they both are (read the Appendix for more on Berkshire Hathaway). There's more than one way to skin this portfolio diversification cat.

What everyone agrees is that you don't want to have all your eggs in one basket. If you have two investments, everyone sees the merit of having them uncorrelated with each another. That is to say, you'll have the smoothest ride if both have good long-term returns, but one is up when the other is down and vice versa. That way, each of their individual peaks and valleys will smooth out the other's, delivering you the pure gold of the returns without the month-to-month volatility usually required to get it.

In the real world, investments that perfectly and profitably hedge each other are impossible to come by. Nevertheless, it's worth trying to get as much diversification as we can. When we own thousands of stocks (as when indexing the market à la Bogle), they're all buzzing up and down but the net effect is that we can collect the honey with a minimum of commotion. A market-wide level of diversification is an extremely diversified portfolio. No one contests this.

A standard diversified equity portfolio today might look something like Figure 4.1.

Figure 4.1: The Apple-Pie Portfolio

MSCI Emerging
Markets Index
5%

MSCI EAFE Index
25%

S&P 500 Index
70%

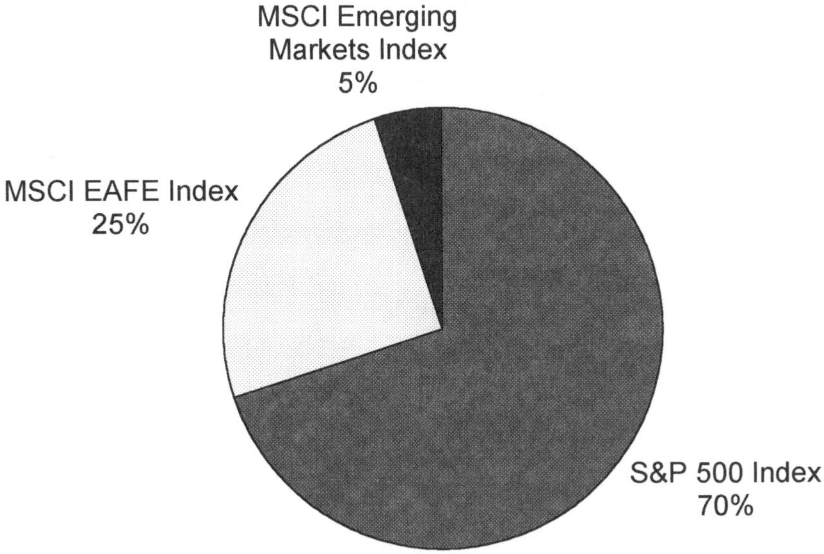

This portfolio is a no-brainer. If you own a GLOM portfolio such as discussed earlier, it would be instructive to compare your performance with this one as a benchmark. What you'll likely find is that this one is better, at least on the equity side and on a risk-adjusted basis. We might call this the "Apple-Pie" portfolio.

Our friend Jeremy Siegel, writing in *The Future for Investors,* has recently advocated raising the foreign exposure to 40 percent, in anticipation of the growth of the world economy outside the U.S. in the coming decades. Perhaps over time this will become the new recipe.

The Global Capitalization–Weighted Portfolio

If we're true believers in the efficiency of global markets, an even better way to assemble a portfolio would be to construct a worldwide, market capitalization–weighted portfolio. This way, we'd own the entire equity market of planet Earth in proportion to the size of the capital markets in each country, effectively indexing within each nation and across borders according to the size of every company's total stock market capitalization (which equals its stock price times the number of shares it has outstanding). This involves harnessing all global investors to our asset-allocation weighing machine.

This isn't a bad bet, considering that these are people who are backing their investment opinions with their money. We'd own more of the companies where investors have put more money, and less of the companies where they've put less. Unfortunately, some countries like China make it very difficult to invest inside their borders, and some nations have such ineffectual or unstable legal systems and markets that we don't feel comfortable parking our simoleons there. Still, this is about as close as we can safely get to omnipresence at present. Not only do we already know what funds to put in this portfolio, we also know how much of each to buy, as shown in Figure 4.2.

Figure 4.2: The Global Capitalization–Weighted Portfolio

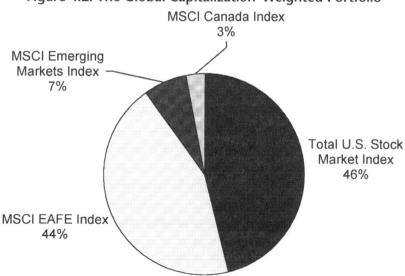

MSCI Canada Index 3%

MSCI Emerging Markets Index 7%

Total U.S. Stock Market Index 46%

MSCI EAFE Index 44%

The total stock market index tracks the Dow Jones Wilshire 5000 Composite Index (or something similar), a cap-weighted index of all the publicly traded companies in the United States. The MSCI EAFE Index does the same for the large capitalization companies in the world's developed markets, while the MSCI Emerging Markets Index follows the 25 countries with developing economies. Canada was never included in the original EAFE index, so we added it here in proportion to its weight in the global economy.

This portfolio spans the globe: We own 2,614 companies in 48 countries controlling some $25 trillion in market capitalization. Short of owning casinos on Venus, that's what we call diversified.

On the other hand, many financial experts would choke on having 54 percent of our assets abroad, in non-dollar-denominated currencies. After all, the mortgage has to be paid in dollars, not yen or euros. Increasingly, though, many things we buy are ultimately paid for in foreign currencies—our Japanese or German cars or our toasters and televisions. Could it just be jingoism that causes us to keep so much of our money under the mattress in the United States?

Behavioral psychologists are forever berating us for what they call the home-team bias: the fact that we tend to overinvest in what's familiar, such as our company stock or the local utility. Maybe the prejudice against having a truly global-weighted portfolio is an example of this xenophobia writ large. Fidelity's Peter Lynch abetted this trend by recommending that investors buy what they know. If you like lattes, buy Starbucks; if you like iPods, buy Apple. We've never really understood this approach. It worked disastrously for Tad, and there seem to be many more Tads than Peter Lynches out there in investorland.

In the end, we have no need to defend this portfolio allocation—the burden of proof for the passive, efficient, market-index-oriented investor really rests with those who advocate anything different. If they recommend only having 30 percent of assets abroad, we might ask: Why this number? Why not 32 percent or 19 percent? Is it because 30 percent worked the best over the last ten years? But why is that relevant? What about the last 6 years—or 17 years? If it's because they don't like having so much in non-dollar-denominated currencies, we have to ask: Why not? Doesn't the market transvalue all currencies? Don't they believe that the market is efficient?

While no one wants to come right out and say so, the fact is that once you move your portfolio away from market capitalization weightings, anything goes. As we hope to show, this can be a *good* thing.

"Bogleheads" Speak

A popular online discussion group hosted by Morningstar called the "Vanguard Diehards" frequently hashes out portfolio-related issues. We fished out a portfolio from their forum's archives for your delectation. As a caveat, we should point out that here, as with many of the canned portfolios we'll be discussing, the "Bogleheads" (as discussion participants call themselves) aren't specifically recommending this portfolio for anyone. They present it for its value as a teaching aid—or some such. Sometimes we wonder if people just give these disclaimers because they don't want anybody blaming them if they lose money.

This particular Diehard Portfolio is certainly better than most. It's shown in Figure 4.3.

Figure 4.3: A Sample Diehard Portfolio

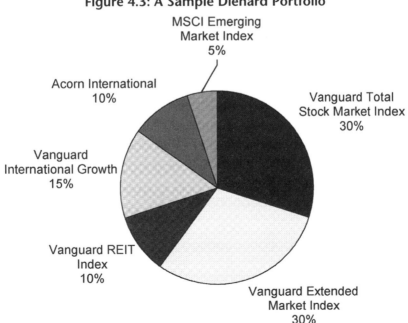

What's notable here is the greater emphasis on smaller capitalization stocks (Vanguard Extended Market Index, Acorn International) than is found in a pure capitalization-weighted portfolio, as well as the addition of Real Estate Investment Trusts (REITs). What's motivating this change? The fact that *small cap stocks and REITs behave as their own independent asset classes even though they're already contained (in smaller quantities) in the total stock market index.*

Whoops! This is a jolting intrusion of Modern Portfolio Theory that's going to take us down a slippery slope away from a strictly capitalization-weighted, efficient-market portfolio to better risk-adjusted returns. Once we cut ourselves loose from the capitalization-weighted model and start increasing our allocation to certain sub-asset classes, the question shifts to: *What are the best assets to add, and in what quantity?*

Modern Portfolio Theory is already implicated in the total stock market indices, of course, in the idea that by seeking a market-wide level of diversification, we earn a high risk-adjusted return. But now we're saying something more. Let's suppose we punch up certain contrary subclasses of stocks within the total global market. We think that owning more of these sub-asset classes will diversify the whole portfolio better than if we just held them in the smaller quantities embedded in the index, because they have a low correlation with the larger index or because they have better risk-adjusted returns, or both. In other words, we can improve on the market-wide return-to-risk ratio by rejiggering our holdings to call out these subsections for special prominence. With this idea, we've crossed the line into the next generation: asset class investing.

(Of course, most GLOM stockholders have the very opposite problem. They own too few stocks or funds that were bought with insufficient attention to their intercorrelations, so they end up with a drastically submarket level of diversification and less than optimal risk-adjusted returns. Folks like these will improve (supercharge?) their portfolios by going to a market-wide level of investing through the use of simple index funds, as we suggested earlier.)

Asset Class Investing

Once asset classes of stocks are identified within the market, we can play them off against each other the way Archie plays Betty against Veronica.

Here's another metaphor for what we're trying to do: Imagine that you're a conductor and want to make music. You put an ad in the paper and invite every musician in your town to show up with their instruments at the park. You could climb on the bandstand and make music conducting them all in unison. "Freebird," anyone?

But there's another approach. You might get out a bullhorn and announce: "You kazoo players and bagpipers—go home! That goes for the accordion players, too. But you guys with the violins, come up here and sit together, and everybody with violas and cellos, too. Woodwinds, over here . . ." And pretty soon you have an orchestra, and you can conduct a Beethoven symphony. In other words, by selecting important subgroups from the class of all musicians to play their own parts, you can make significantly better music than you did before.

A different conductor might send home the strings but keep the guys with Fender Telecasters and Ludwig drums. Another might keep a jazz pianist, saxophonist, and double-bass player. Through careful selection and specialization of roles, a variety of musical styles can be achieved to suit the conductor's purposes.

The same holds true with portfolios. Let's take a close look at how the interaction of specialized portfolio components can work together to make music that is more beautiful to the investor's ears.

Break It Down

Look at a correlation table for three asset classes we just encountered in the Diehard's portfolio, shown in Table 4.1.

Table 4.1: Correlation Matrix 1979–2006			
	S&P 500	Small Cap	REITs
S&P 500	1		
Small Cap	0.80	1	
REITs	0.49	0.62	1

This table shows the correlation among these three asset classes, which is to say, how much their prices have varied with each other over the past three years on a monthly basis. In theory, correlations can run anywhere from plus 1 (a perfect positive correlation, as each of these asset classes correlates perfectly with itself) to minus 1 (a perfect negative correlation). The correlation of small cap stocks with the S&P 500 is fairly high (0.80), but the real beauty comes from adding REITs. They have only a moderate correlation with both the S&P 500 (0.49) and small cap stocks (0.62). The expensive word that springs to mind here is *orthogonal.* We're looking for asset classes that are as orthogonal as possible—that is, that have a low correlation to each other and move independently. This gives Modern Portfolio Theory the elbow room it needs to work its magic.

Does it work? Consult Table 4.2.

Table 4.2: Returns and S.D.s 2002–2006			
Asset Class	Ticker	Returns	S.D.
S&P 500	VFINX	6.7%	12.4%
Small Cap	VEXMX	12.3%	14.3%
REITs	VGSIX	21.6%	14.2%
Average		13.5%	13.7%
Actual		13.5%	11.7%

Table 4.2 shows the returns, standard deviations, and Return/Risk ratios for each of the same three asset classes considered separately and then, on the bottom line, taken together. If you'd invested an equal amount of money in all three asset classes beginning in 2002, you might expect that by 2006 you would have earned their average returns (13.5 percent) with their average volatility (13.7 percent). But check out the last line: In practice, you got all the average returns (13.5 percent) *but at much less than their average standard deviation* (11.7 percent instead of 13.7 percent). The risk-adjusted returns for the portfolio containing all three assets was significantly better than just taking them averaged together.

If you were unfamiliar with the power of Modern Portfolio Theory up until now, we hope you'll stop and thank the Almighty for this great gift—the biggest free lunch in financial economics. If it hasn't already, it's going change the way you invest. If you've been skimming through this discussion while waiting to get to the centerfold, please go back and make sure you understand this example. It's the acorn of this book in a nutshell. *Investors pursue their dreams of beating the market through such futile means as individual stock picking, short-term market timing, and momentum investing, yet they ignore the one strategy that reliably offers market-beating risk-adjusted returns: massive diversification within and among asset classes. It's money for nothing (but not, alas, chicks for free).*

This increased diversification benefit is the motivation behind the Diehard's portfolio. Note that they have done the same trick with foreign stocks, combining large cap (VIGRX) and small cap (ACINX) in foreign developed markets. Then they play off developed with emerging markets and foreign stocks with U.S. stocks, to further diversify their equity holdings. The net result is a portfolio that's more diversified than the capitalization-weighted global stock market, as paradoxical as that might sound. We greatly hesitate to employ the cliché about the whole being greater than the sum of its parts, and we're even more reluctant to breathe the word *synergy,* but there it is.

Let's look at some other canned portfolios that employ this same technique.

Scott Burns

Scott Burns, a mild-mannered newspaper reporter for the great metropolitan *Dallas Morning News,* coined the Couch Potato portfolio that your authors extolled in our previous epic, *Yes, You Can Still Retire Comfortably!* The reason we love it so much is that it holds only two funds, has very low expenses, and yet provides a high degree of diversification. We're morally certain that it's far better than most GLOM portfolios out there in Duckberg. As Burns writes: "If you can divide by two on a calculator, you can be a Couch Potato portfolio manager." His updated Couch Potato portfolio is presented in Figure 4.4.

Figure 4.4: The Couch Potato Portfolio

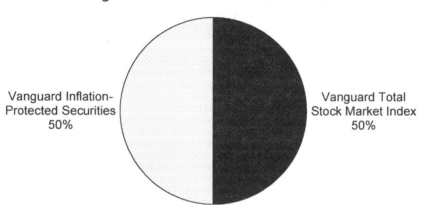

Vanguard Inflation-Protected Securities 50%

Vanguard Total Stock Market Index 50%

Burns offers his readers a set of progressive variations on this basic theme, each one further diversifying the portfolio before it by adding one more asset class. His Margarita portfolio (Figure 4.5) adds Vanguard's Total International Stock Market, which includes the MSCI EAFE as well as a small holding of the MSCI Emerging Markets Index. This diversifies away from the U.S. market-centrism of the couch potato portfolio.

Figure 4.5: The Margarita Portfolio

Vanguard Inflation-
Protected Securities
33.3%

Vanguard Total
Stock Market Index
33.3%

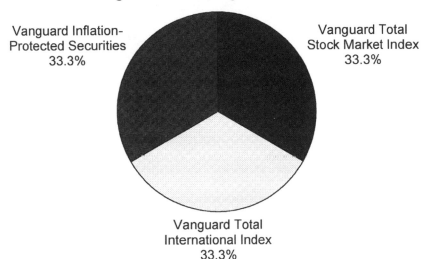

Vanguard Total
International Index
33.3%

To be fair, this portfolio originated in an 1996 article in *Kiplinger's* magazine. It was later called the "Cold Shower" portfolio in *The Wall Street Journal.* "There may be better investment strategies," John Bogle said of it, "but the number of strategies that are worse are infinite."

Want still more diversification? Burns suggests the Four Square portfolio (Figure 4.6), which adds the American Century International Bond Fund to the mix. This takes us back to a 50 percent stock/50 percent bond allocation, with half of our stocks and bonds in the U.S. and half abroad.

Figure 4.6: The Four Square Portfolio

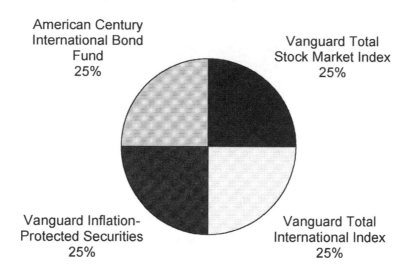

American Century International Bond Fund 25%

Vanguard Total Stock Market Index 25%

Vanguard Inflation-Protected Securities 25%

Vanguard Total International Index 25%

Burns's Five-Fold portfolio (Figure 4.7) finally gets around to adding REITs to the picture.

Figure 4.7: The Five-Fold Portfolio

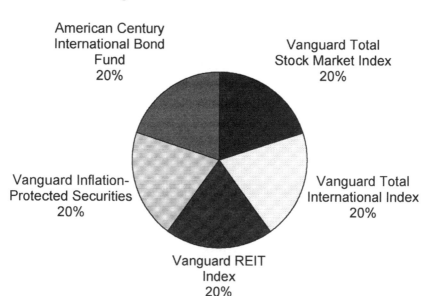

American Century International Bond Fund 20%

Vanguard Total Stock Market Index 20%

Vanguard Inflation-Protected Securities 20%

Vanguard Total International Index 20%

Vanguard REIT Index 20%

Finally, Burns finishes the course with his "Six Ways from Sunday" portfolio, shown in Figure 4.8. This time he adds another real asset, energy, as a diversifier.

Figure 4.8: The Six Ways from Sunday Portfolio

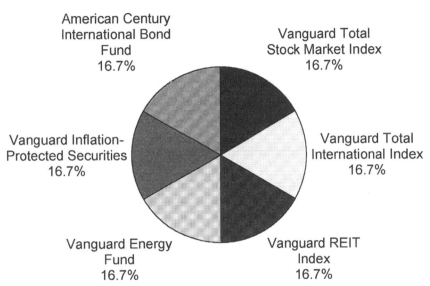

American Century
International Bond
Fund
16.7%

Vanguard Total
Stock Market Index
16.7%

Vanguard Inflation-
Protected Securities
16.7%

Vanguard Total
International Index
16.7%

Vanguard Energy
Fund
16.7%

Vanguard REIT
Index
16.7%

In reviewing the Burns portfolios, the presumption is that more asset classes is better because they afford greater diversification. That gives us a better risk-adjusted return over time, *if* we can handle the complexity. If we're better at just dividing by two on our calculator, then maybe we should stick with the Couch Potato. His "Six Ways from Sunday" portfolio actually has the best return/risk ratio over the past four years (on the equity side) of all the portfolios we present here, because its big bets on REITs and energy paid off like a slot machine. Burns, however, would be the first to caution that this is no guarantee of future performance.

Coward's Portfolio

Our pal, the redoubtable William Bernstein of Efficient Frontier Advisors, proposed the Coward's portfolio (Figure 4.9) back in 1996.

He called it thusly because it hedges by putting half of its stocks in the U.S. and half abroad.

Figure 4.9: The Coward's Portfolio

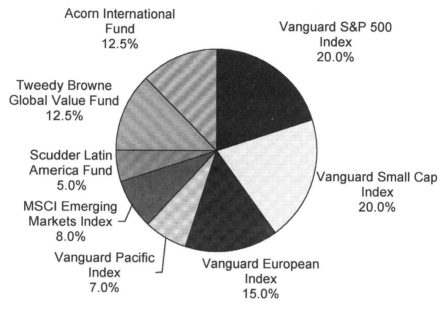

Notice how, in addition to the small versus large cap and the domestic versus foreign play-offs, Bernstein has introduced some regional competition: Europe versus Pacific; emerging markets versus developed; and, with the Tweedy Browne Global Value fund, value versus growth. This portfolio has been very successful and is all the more commendable for having the courage to play the "value" card when value was out of favor with investors.

Let's look at two more examples before sounding off further.

Coffeehouse Portfolio

Investment advisor Bill Schultheis has written a book we haven't read called *The Coffeehouse Investor* which espouses the portfolio in Figure 4.10.

Figure 4.10: The Coffeehouse Portfolio

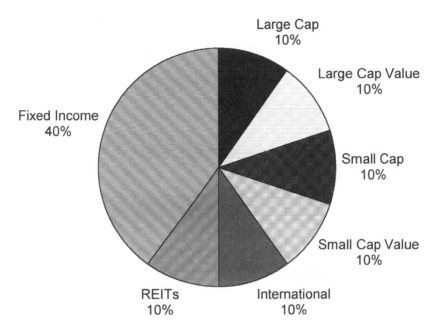

This portfolio, in addition to stock/bond, domestic/international, and REITs, also plays off big stocks against small and value stocks against growth stocks.

Four Corners Portfolio

Here's another portfolio that's up to the same trick, even more starkly: A very simple method that captures the entire United States stock market but slices and dices it into four constituent quadrants, it's called the "Four Corners" portfolio. It owns four index funds in equal weighting: large cap growth, large cap value, small cap growth, and small cap value, as shown in Figure 4.11.

Figure 4.11: The Four Corners Portfolio

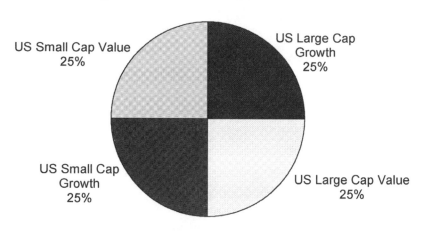

US Small Cap Value
25%

US Large Cap
Growth
25%

US Small Cap
Growth
25%

US Large Cap Value
25%

Where do these two pairs of antagonists (big/small and value/growth) come from?

The Fama-French Factors

In the 1980s, two economics professors (Eugene Fama and Ken French) did a factor analysis of historical stock market returns and discovered that two variables account for most of the differences in returns across equity portfolios. These factors are: the market capitalization of the companies held and where they fall along the value versus growth continuum.

Market capitalization is easy to measure: just multiply the number of shares a company has outstanding by today's market price. What Fama and French discovered was that small capitalization companies tended to have higher returns than large cap companies; these upstarts tend to have better earnings potential than their more mature brethren. At the same time, they're riskier—they have higher volatility. So the market compensates the owners (the shareholders) of these companies by paying them a higher return over time.

This doesn't happen all the time, of course. There can be stretches that last for years and years when small cap stocks underperform large cap stocks. But over the long run, the former are slightly further out on the return/risk dimension than the latter: greater returns trading off against greater risks. Best of all, for reasons no one has definitively explained, their extra returns seem to be slightly greater than their extra risks.

The other, and more pronounced, Fama-French finding was that value stocks outperform growth stocks. Value stocks are those that sell at a low price relative to their fundamentals (earnings, dividends, book values, and so on), while growth stocks are more glamorous companies whose shares sell at a premium to their earnings, but with the embedded prospect of their earnings growing at a much faster clip.

Value companies are often in some distress. Perhaps they're past their prime or they've fallen on hard times. Perhaps they service a mature market with a constant demand but with no real growth prospects. Over time, surprisingly, they tend to outperform growth stocks—the exact opposite of what one might expect. Again, there's no definitive explanation of why value stocks win. While they display both greater returns and volatility, their returns outpace their volatility.

The Fama-French findings were initially met with skepticism, but further research using out-of-sample time periods and foreign markets has confirmed the validity of the small cap and value premiums. Fama and French went on to form their own investment company, Dimensional Fund Advisors (DFA), which caters to institutional and high-networth investors and has become a cult in the brainiac investing world. Meanwhile, the value and size dimensions they uncovered have been memorialized in the "style boxes" that Morningstar uses to map every mutual fund.

The Fama-French insight has proven so trenchant that, once we know where a given mutual fund falls on the value/growth and small cap/large cap axis, and then subtract the drag on performance due to the dead weight of its cash holdings and management fees, we can predict its returns with jaw-dropping precision. Whatever "Arabian Nights" tales that active fund managers weave to hold investors in their thrall, in practice their returns seem to be largely dictated by a simple linear regression formula.

When we combine an ordinary stock market portfolio such as the S&P 500 with the asset classes of small cap and value stocks, we get a resulting portfolio with returns that are higher than those of the S&P

500. Meanwhile, on the risk side, the volatility of holding the stock market, the small cap, and the value asset classes cancel each other out to some degree. This means that through resourceful tinkering, we can move the furniture around inside the portfolio until it gives us better expected returns for the same level of expected volatility. By mixing value and small cap stocks to a market portfolio, Fama and French capture the diversification free lunch.

Fundamental Indexing

More recently, we've heard about new ways of indexing the markets that have been developed to weight the portfolio using some principle other than the market capitalization of the component stocks. This is called "fundamental indexing." They use dividend yields, price-to-book ratios, price/earnings ratios, or even just counting (as with an equal-weighted index) to sort and then proportionately invest in the stocks. Voilà: The resulting index looks like it gets better returns than the old-fashioned, cap-weighted index.

The problem is that all these valuation-sorted indexes have the effect of pushing the portfolios in a small cap and value direction, shooting the curl down precisely the same wave that Fama and French surfed to shore long ago. It's far from evident at this point that any of these approaches adds anything new, beyond a pretext to launch another raft of investment products—not that there's anything wrong with that. Over time, some of them will undoubtedly prove quite useful.

Where We Are

We've looked at a bunch of different portfolios cooked up by various experts. These portfolios attempt to achieve diversification benefits by pitting low-correlated asset classes against each other. By doing so, they should garner small improvements to their risk-adjusted returns that, over the years, could compound into large differences in the pile of money in our money bins.

Table 4.3 outlines some interesting features of the portfolios we've just reviewed. Since we already discussed how bonds are only included to suppress volatility, we've removed them from the allocations and here just examine the equity engines, the parts that really deliver the returns.

Table 4.3: Portfolio Equity-Only Characteristics, 2002–2006						
	HISTORICAL			EXPECTED		
Portfolio	Returns	S.D.	Returns/ S.D.	Returns	S.D.	Returns/ S.D.
Apple Pie	9.7%	12.5%	78%	10.7%	15.4%	69%
Global Cap-Weighted	12.6%	12.8%	98%	11.0%	16.1%	68%
Couch Potato	8.0%	12.5%	64%	10.3%	15.2%	68%
Margarita	8.2%	10.1%	81%	8.8%	12.1%	73%
Four-Square	8.2%	10.1%	81%	8.8%	12.1%	73%
Five-Fold	12.6%	9.8%	129%	9.6%	12.9%	74%
Six Ways from Sunday	15.7%	10.3%	152%	10.6%	14.0%	76%
Diehard	13.6%	12.6%	108%	10.7%	14.7%	73%
Coward	14.8%	13.2%	112%	11.3%	15.9%	71%
Coffeehouse	13.2%	12.6%	106%	11.1%	16.0%	70%
Four Corners	11.0%	13.4%	82%	11.3%	17.2%	66%

Let's meditate on this table for a minute. After all, these are some of the best portfolios out there. On the left, we have the historical annual average returns, the standard deviations, and the ratio between the returns and standard deviations for each of these portfolios for the recent period from 2002 through 2006. The returns are important, because that's why we hold the portfolio in the first place. And the return-to-risk ratio is important because it sheds light on our risk-adjusted returns. The higher this figure is, the less we'll have to add in the way of performance-compromising bonds to get the results we want.

On the right, we see how the Monte Carlo simulator has adjusted the forward-looking expectations from these portfolios. The period from 2002 to 2006 was one of extremely low market volatility. It has boosted the expected *future* volatility to something closer to long-term norms; it has also flattened out the differences in returns of the portfolios going forward. The most promising portfolios look to be those that are more complicated, probably because these are the ones that snare the free diversification benefit.

Interlude

If we set the books aside, take the dog for a walk, light a Montecristo, and blow a few smoke rings while watching the sun set over the Pacific, what strikes us is that, from one point of view, these portfolios are all really about the same. While they're a big improvement over the GLOM portfolios most folks hold by default, they're nonetheless all variants of what we might call—for lack of a more elegant term—the GLOB portfolio: the great global glob of stocks.

These portfolios remind us (and admittedly, we're reaching here) of those lame, tame rock 'n' roll covers sung by pretty white boys in the 1950s: They don't really reach into the deep boogie-woogie soul of Modern Portfolio Theory. As great as they are, what all these portfolios have in common is that they are significantly *underdiversified*. They need a shot of rhythm and blues.

What? Undiversified? With a half-dozen asset classes? Are we crazy?

Don't Stop!

So far, we've seen that the big idea is to diversify by pitting asset classes against each other: REITs, foreign stocks, small cap stocks, value stocks, and the like. But why stop there? Investors have been offered a free lunch of portfolio diversification, but they've settled for a carrot stick on the veranda when they could be inside the banquet hall eating steak.

Within the thousands of global companies that all these portfolios contain, there are sectors or subgroups that travel (like Linda Ronstadt and the Stone Poneys) to the beat of a different drum. These include energy stocks, utilities, technology, commodities, health care, and other market sectors. There are also individual countries where we might benefit from staking out a bigger position. And, heresy of heresies, there are even individual stocks that might diversify the whole lot of them better than any mutual fund can.

Now, we're not saying that we have a crystal ball and can identify the top-performing sectors, countries, or stocks going forward. Only *Mad Money's* Jim Cramer can do that. Just kidding! No one can. Our claim is far more modest. We're going to examine those sectors, countries, and companies that have the lowest correlations with our other GLOB holdings, and then add these like a drop of vermouth to sex up the cocktail.

Let's start with the assets that have the lowest correlation with the S&P 500 Index. This index is going to play a significant role in nearly every portfolio. It broadly accesses the large capitalization stocks of the United States. Because it's so widely used, it can be accessed cheaply (SPY and IVV both track it and charge a mere 0.10% in expenses annually, for example). We'll use it as a general proxy for the GLOB portfolio. If you want to use a different index, be our guest.

Table 4.4 shows some sectors that have lower correlations with the S&P 500 than most.

Table 4.4: Sector Correlations to S&P 500 2002–2006		
Sector	Ticker	r
S&P 500 Index	SPY	1
Dow Jones U.S. Telecommunications	IYZ	0.83
Goldman Sachs Networking	IGN	0.81
Dow Jones U.S. Consumer Goods	IYK	0.68
Dow Jones U.S. Utilities	IDU	0.60
Goldman Sachs Natural Resources	IGE	0.55
Dow Jones U.S. Energy	IYE	0.49
Cohen & Steers Realty Majors	ICF	0.42
Gold	^GOX	0.18
AIG Commodity Index	^DJC	0.02

We also might want to add some individual countries. Table 4.5 shows some that have lower correlations to the U.S. market than the EAFE or Emerging Markets indexes.

Table 4.5: Country Correlations to S&P 500 2002–2006

Fund	Ticker	r
S&P 500 Index Fund	SPY	1
MSCI EAFE Index	EFA	0.82
MSCI Emerging Markets Index	EEM	0.78
MSCI Belgium Index Fund	EWK	0.73
MSCI South Korea Index Fund	EWY	0.72
MSCI Australia Index Fund	EWA	0.69
MSCI Singapore Index Fund	EWS	0.67
MSCI Taiwan Index Fund	EWT	0.65
MSCI Brazil Index Fund	EWZ	0.65
MSCI Hong Kong Index Fund	EWH	0.61
MSCI Austria Index Fund	EWO	0.48
MSCI Malaysia Index Fund	EWM	0.43
MSCI Japan Index Fund	EWJ	0.38

Of Names and Things

Notice that the EAFE index and even the Emerging Markets have fairly high correlations to the S&P 500 index. Here we come to a major fault line running between advocates of capitalization-weighted portfolios and Modern Portfolio Theorists. From an efficient-market, cap-weighted perspective, globalization is essential. From a Modern Portfolio Theory point of view, however, globalization is ineffective. It appears to offer a great deal of diversity to U.S.-based portfolios, but in practice people investing abroad for diversification are kidding themselves if they think that they're doing much good.

Plato encouraged his followers to look beyond the realm of opinion to the underlying mathematical reality. We're misled by the names and labels of the funds we own to blithely assume we hold diversified investments, when in fact we only own a bunch of different *names* of investments. Diversification is a function of the *behavior* of the constituent parts of our portfolio, and nothing else. We see a sign for the Matterhorn and assume we're in Switzerland, when in fact we're only visiting Disneyland. This brings us to a fundamental problem with many portfolios today: *pseudo-diversification*. It's far easier for Wall Street to manufacture funds with different names than it is to create funds that are meaningfully different in the way they perform.

All this gaseous, theory-driven talk about what we should hold in our portfolio leads to suboptimal allocation decisions. Moreover, this loss is invisible, because we never see the dollars that aren't in our bank accounts because we didn't diversify more extensively in the first place. Until we take the trouble to analyze our portfolios, we're in the dark. This is why we need portfolio management tools like the QPP Monte Carlo simulator, which lays out the correlations among the individual assets, as well as showing their correlation to the portfolio as a whole.

It makes a certain amount of sense that holding both the S&P 500 Index and some basic commodity such as gold or oil could work. One could argue that a high price for oil puts a damper on the entire U.S. economy, or that high inflation affects the price of oil and gold positively but hits the stock market negatively. Why the Malaysian stock market should have a lower correlation to the U.S. stock market is less immediately clear. There might be a good reason for it, or it might be just a coincidence.

Whenever a high or low correlation is discovered, people will always be able to make up the reasons why it exists—after the fact. Instead of using a theory to make a prediction about what we should consider using in our portfolios, we're generally better off to let the numbers do the talking.

Are Correlations Forever?

As wonderful as it is to find assets with low correlations to each other, remember that these relationships aren't cast in stone. Assets moving in opposite directions for years can change on a dime and start moving in tandem. How are we to deal with this?

We certainly don't want to discard the correlations. Doing so will leave us with portfolio simulations that assume zero correlation of the underlying assets, and these in turn would lead us to woefully underestimate our total risk.

Highly divergent assets may move more in tandem going forward than they did in the past. That is basic regression to the mean. Even so, *we're better off choosing from a pool of less correlated assets with the assumption that we may need to account for a little more risk, than choosing from a pool of highly correlated assets and hoping that they grow apart.* The fact that on a bad day many asset classes will all fall down doesn't mean we should just forget about correlation and go to the beach. To the contrary, it means that we need to seek out every drop of low correlation that we can. If your fortunes depend on what the stock market does over any given one-day time period, you shouldn't be invested in stocks at all.

Can We Do Better?

To diversify a portfolio of S&P 500 stocks, we won't just add assets as if a low correlation were all that mattered. We really have three balls in the air, and we have to keep our eye on all of them: the correlations of the assets, their risks, and their returns. If we add an asset that has a low correlation to the S&P 500 but its risks are too high, it could still lower the risk-adjusted returns in spite of the low correlation; gold might be an example of this. On the other hand, if we add an asset whose returns are low, it could drag the whole portfolio down, even if its correlation and risks were also low. Here, a prime example would be cash.

What we really want is a special subclass of assets: those tickers providing both diversification *and* improvement in the reward-to-risk profile of the resulting portfolio. Where on earth could we mortals ever hope to get our hands on such a coveted list of superdesirable diversifying investment opportunities that might benefit virtually any GLOB portfolio? From Table 4.6, that's where.

Table 4.6: GLOB Portfolio Diversifiers

Company	Ticker	Industry
Aflac	AFL	Insurance
Anheuser-Busch	BUD	Beverage
Avery Dennison	AVY	Paper
BB&T	BBT	Banking
BCE	BCE	Telecommunications
Colonial Properties	CLP	REIT
Clorox	CLX	Household Products
ConAgra	CAG	Food Manufacturing
Constellation Brands	STZ	Beverage
Chesapeake Utilities	CPK	Gas Utility
Powershares Commodity ETF	DBC	Commodities
DTE Energy Holdings	DTE	Electric Utility
Consolidated Edison	ED	Electric Utility
Enbridge	ENB	Natural Gas
Hormel	HRL	Food Manufacturing
iShares Japan Fund	EWJ	Japan
iShares Malaysia Fund	EWM	Malaysia
Exponent	EXPO	Engineering/ Construction
FTI Consulting	FCN	Consulting
FirstEnergy	FE	Electric Utility
General Mills	GIS	Food Manufacturing
Gold ETF	IAU	Precious Metals
Cohen & Steers Realty Majors	ICF	REIT Index
Utility ETF	IDU	Utilities

Table 4.6: GLOB Portfolio Diversifiers (cont'd.)

Company	Ticker	Industry
Natural Resources ETF	IGE	Natural Resources
Energy ETF	IYE	Energy
Johnson & Johnson	JNJ	Drugs
Kellogg	K	Food Manufacturing
Kimberly-Clark	KMB	Household Products
Lockheed-Martin	LMT	Aerospece/Defense
Lexington Corp. Properties	LXP	REIT
Municipal Mortgage	MMA	Finance
New Jersey Resources	NJR	Gas Utility
Northrop Grumman	NOC	Aerospace/Defense
Novartis AG ADR	NVS	Drugs
Northwest Natural Gas	NWN	Oil & Gas
Public Service Enterprises	PEG	Electric Utility
PepsiCo	PEP	Beverage
Proctor & Gamble	PG	Personal Products
Southern Company	SO	Electric Utility
Southwest Gas	SWX	Gas Utility
United Utilities	UUPLY	Water Utility
Valero Energy	VLO	Oil/Gas
Washington Mutual	WM	Savings & Loan
Waters	WAT	Medical Equipment
WGL Holdings	WGL	Gas Utility
Wyeth	WYE	Drugs

Let's quickly backpedal and say that these are candidates for inclusion in your portfolio and that you will have to do your own due diligence to assure that they're still viable at the time you're reading this. We made an effort to include securities that had some underlying merit, at least as of the time of this writing: reasonable price-to-earnings ratios, a history of earnings, liquidity, stability, and so on. Surely there are many other companies that would be great diversifiers that we've failed to identify here, but at least this is a starting point. The securities in Table 4.6 are the nuts and bolts that we'll use to supercharge your portfolio, starting in the very next chapter.

Chapter Five

Step 5: Use the Monte Carlo Simulator to Test-Drive Your Portfolio

The Monte Carlo simulator is the better mousetrap investors need to analyze their portfolios. You can download a free trial of the Quantext QPP Monte Carlo simulator that works with Microsoft Excel from **www.quantext.com**. There's also an online Monte Carlo simulator at **www.financialengines.com** and rudimentary versions are available at the Websites of some brokerage firms such as Fidelity and T. Rowe Price. There are undoubtedly many others out there as well. Unfortunately, not all Monte Carlo simulators are created equal. We happen to like the feature set on the Quantext QPP simulator and will be using it in the examples that follow.

Our exact findings aren't particularly important. What *is* important is that you understand the method, so you can mix your own concoctions at home.

Your Portfolio Becomes One with the Universe

The core of your portfolio is simply a machine to harvest the profits from global capital markets. All that's required is a large scoop (such as an index fund) to cheaply and reliably vacuum up all those nickels and dimes from companies all over the world and deposit them into our accounts.

While at first blush the approach we espouse may remind casual readers of the "Core & Explore" approach extolled by the financial services industry, our approach is really the opposite. The idea of Core & Explore is that you have your core portfolio in something boring and humdrum like a low-expense, passive S&P 500 index fund, but then seek greater glory by adding some actively managed investments that promise to spike the punch.

By contrast, the additions we propose are all made with an eye to enhancing the core and making it more productive and efficient. It might just be called "Core" or "Core & Score" (but not by us). By diversifying the core as fully as possible, it becomes everything it can be. Some examples should make this clear.

Portfolio #1: Apple Pie à la Mode

Let's start with the 70 percent total U.S. stock market index, 25 percent MSCI Europe, Australia, and Far East index, and 5 percent MSCI emerging markets index we started with in the last chapter. The first order of business is to pick some mutual funds with a sufficient history of operations (at least three years) that represent these asset classes and enter their tickers into the QPP Monte Carlo simulator. These indexes are tracked very closely by several mutual funds: Vanguard's Total Stock Market Index Fund (VTSMX), Fidelity's EAFE Index Fund (FSIIX), and Vanguard's Emerging Markets Index Fund (VEIEX).

Next, we send QPP online to grab three years' worth of data from which to base our calculations. As the Apple Pie portfolio stands, it has a projected return of 11.2 percent against a standard deviation of 17 percent, for a reward-to-risk ratio of 0.66, as shown in Figure 5.1.

Figure 5.1: The Apple Pie Portfolio

Fund Name	Percentage of Funds	Average Annual Return	Expected Annual Return	Expected Standard Deviation
Total Stock Market	70.0%	11.10%	11.2%	17.0%
Foreign Developed Market	25.0%	10.51%		
Emerging Market Index	5.0%	17.07%		
–	0.0%	–		
–	0.0%	–		
–	0.0%	–		
–	0.0%	–		
–	0.0%	–		
–	0.0%	–		
–	0.0%	–		
–	0.0%	–		
–	0.0%	–		
–	0.0%	–		
–	0.0%	–		
–	0.0%	–		
–	0.0%	–		
–	0.0%	–		
–	0.0%	–		

Historical Data

Start: 12/31/2003   End: 12/31/2006

Average Annual Return	Standard Deviation (Annual)
13.7%	8.1%

Historical Beta: 112.6%
Historical Yield: 1.8%
Portfolio R^2: 91.2%

Performance of S&P 500 over historical period

Avg. Ann. Return S&P 500 (no dividends) 8.4%

Annual Standard Deviation on S&P 500 6.9%

We might as well pause here for a moment and review some of what we're looking at in Figure 5.1, since we'll be seeing much more just like it in the pages ahead. This is a "screen shot" from the QPP Monte Carlo Simulator. On the left-hand side, it lists the asset classes we're examining and the percentage of each in the portfolio. Next to it is the Monte Carlo simulator's projected forward-looking return for each security.

On the right-hand side are several sets of measures. At the top is the portfolio's projected returns, based on this Monte Carlo simulator's distributions of the future performance scenarios. Below that is shown the historical total returns (dividends plus capital appreciation) of the portfolio over the specified time period, in this case, from December 31, 2003 to December 31, 2006. It is worth noting that the expected future volatility is much higher than the historical volatility.

At the bottom of the right-hand side of Figure 5.1 are a few other measures we can safely ignore for now but that we'll come back to later. Just for the record, *beta* is a measure of the volatility of this portfolio compared with that of the S&P 500 Index. A beta of 100 percent indicates that its volatility moves in tandem with the market. A beta of less than 100 percent indicates that the portfolio dampens the volatility of the market. In this case, the beta of 112.6% indicates that adding foreign developed and emerging markets to the S&P 500 results in a portfolio that's even more volatile than the U.S. market taken by itself.

The next metric presented is the historical yield. This shows the payout, expressed as a percentage of the underlying price, of dividends or coupons of the underlying securities over the time period that we sampled. We'll spend a chapter later on the implications of Monte Carlo simulation for income investing.

The final metric is something esoteric called *R-squared*. This figure can range from zero to 100 percent and describes how much of the underlying portfolio's behavior is explained by movements in the S&P 500 alone. In this case, we have a portfolio composed 70 percent of the S&P 500 Index, and yet 91 percent of its movement is a function of the movement of the S&P 500. This shows how international diversification isn't all it's cracked up to be. We'll revisit the concept of R-squared in more detail later on when we discuss hedge funds.

To resume: Can we improve the performance of the Apple Pie portfolio? Let's enter the tickers of ten mutual funds from Table 4.6 that we think might diversify it further. These are: commodities (DBC), gold (IAU), energy (IYE), utilities (IDU), Japan (EWJ), Malaysia (EWM), natural resources (IGE), and real estate (ICF). But wait—two of these funds, DJP and IAU, have only opened recently, so we have no history on them from which the Monte Carlo simulator can extrapolate. So instead of DJP, we'll enter ^DJC, the ticker for the AIG commodities index, and then decrement (decrease incrementally) its performance by 0.75 percent annually to account for the fees that the fund charges but the index doesn't. Instead of IAU or GLD—the gold ETFs—we'll use the Vanguard Precious Metals and Mining Fund (VGPMX) as a proxy. As the ads said about the Broadway show *Beatlemania,* it's not the Beatles, but an incredible simulation. We're not seeking perfection here; pretty good answers will be plenty good enough. Table 5.1 shows the correlations of all these asset classes to the Apple Pie portfolio.

Table 5.1: Apple Pie Portfolio Correlations 2003–2006	
Total US Stock Market	0.97
MSCI EAFE Index	0.89
Emerging Market Index	0.86
Precious Metals	0.65
Malaysia	0.53
Natural Resources	0.54
REITs	0.52
Japan	0.52
Energy	0.46
Utilities	0.36
Commodities	0.18

The first thing we notice is that the three components of the portfolio—the total U.S. stock market, the EAFE index, and the emerging market index—all have high correlations to the performance of the whole group. This is a sign that the portfolio is ripe for improvement.

As we scan down the list of the funds we've added, the general idea is to toss out the ones that have the highest correlations and keep the ones that have the lowest correlations to the portfolio, at least as an initial screen. We see that commodities (^DJC), gold (VGPMX), energy (IYE), utilities (IDU), Malaysia (EWM), and commercial real estate (ICF) all have correlations of less than 0.70 to the portfolio. Since gold and energy are subspecies of commodities, we'll just use commodities for the broadest bet, since it also has the lowest correlation of the bunch.

Next, we chopped the Apple Pie allocation down to 80 percent of its previous size to make headroom for the supercharger. We experimented with adding different funds, first singly and then in combination, and looked at how different amounts changed the expected risks and returns. After some trial and error, we decided to add 5 percent each of commodities, utilities, Malaysia, and REITs. The resulting portfolio looks like Figure 5.2.

Figure 5.2: Apple Pie Portfolio à La Mode

Fund Name	Percentage of Funds	Average Annual Return	Expected Annual Return	Expected Standard Deviation
Total Stock Market	56.0%	11.10%	12.0%	16.0%
Foreign Developed Market	20.0%	10.51%		
Emerging Market Index	4.0%	17.07%	Historical Data	
Commodities	5.0%	17.69%	Start: 12/31/2003	End: 12/31/2006
Utilities	5.0%	12.48%		
REITs	5.0%	12.39%	Average Annual Return	Standard Deviation (Annual)
Malaysia	5.0%	18.60%	14.4%	7.8%
–	0.0%	–		
–	0.0%	–	Historical Beta: 103.1%	
–	0.0%	–	Historical Yield: 2.0%	
–	0.0%	–	Portfolio R^2: 83.5%	
–	0.0%	–		
–	0.0%	–	Performance of S&P 500 over historical period	
–	0.0%	–	Avg. Ann. Return S&P 500 (no dividends) 8.4%	
–	0.0%	–		
–	0.0%	–	Annual Standard Deviation on S&P 500 6.9%	
–	0.0%	–		

67

It now has a projected return of 12 percent annually, versus 11.2 percent for the original formula. The standard deviation has dropped from 17 percent to 16 percent. The reward-to-risk profile has jumped from 0.66 to 0.75, tantalizing us with more returns for less risk. Figure 5.3 puts the improvement in graphic form.

Figure 5.3: Return/Risk Profile of the Apple Pie Portfolios

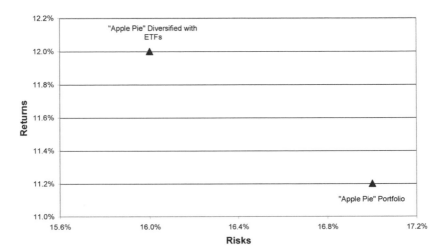

Objection!

But wait! Maybe we haven't improved our portfolio at all, but only pseudo-improved it by adding assets that have outperformed it recently; and then deluded ourselves by projecting this improvement into the future with a smug, pseudo-scientific gloss. If and when these hot asset classes regress to the mean, the supercharger will turn into a net drag on performance, not an enhancement.

Certainly it's possible that commodities and commercial real estate are overdue to cool their heels for a while. Monte Carlo simulation isn't an insurance policy; it's a tool for making intelligent asset allocation decisions. However, if we trim back the expected performance of these asset classes to that of the Apple Pie portfolio before we added them, the portfolio is still improved by their presence. The projected reward-to-risk ratio goes up, but just not quite as much: to 0.71 instead of 0.75.

Here's another way of testing it: Sample a different time period. Instead of looking forward, let's go back to those thrilling days of yesteryear, the disastrous period from March 2000 to March 2003. We have to make a couple of substitutions, because neither our utility fund (IDU) nor our REIT fund (ICF) date back that far. So we'll plug in Van Kampen's Utility Fund (VKUCX) and Vanguard's REIT index fund (VGSIX) in their place.

The Apple Pie portfolio was down 16.4 percent a year during this period, with a standard deviation of 15 percent. With the four additional asset classes added, the portfolio was only down 13.2 percent a year with a standard deviation of 13.1 percent. The more diversified portfolio worked in a different and very difficult time period to provide at least some measure of downside amelioration.

Bonds—Add Bonds

All that remains is to add bonds to suit our risk requirements. As a baseline, let's use the standard 60 percent equity/40 percent bond allocation, and arbitrarily say that this is the risk profile that we want to match. We'll execute it using the Apple Pie portfolio as the base and Vanguard's Short-Term Bond Index fund (VBISX) on the fixed-income side. This portfolio gives us a projected return of about 8.7 percent against a standard deviation of about 10.5 percent.

Now we want to achieve that same level of risk—the same standard deviation, in other words—using our new portfolio. Since our updated hybrid is lower risk to begin with, we discover that we can get to the same place in the risk column by adding less in the way of performance-subtracting bonds. Allocating 37 percent to the bond fund (instead of 40 percent as before) plants us at approximately the same level of standard deviation. The resulting portfolio is shown in Figure 5.4.

Figure 5.4: Adding Bonds to Lower Volatility

Fund Name	Percentage of Funds	Average Annual Return	Expected Annual Return	Expected Standard Deviation
Total Stock Market	35.8%	11.10%	9.5%	10.5%
Foreign Developed Market	12.8%	10.51%		
Emerging Market Index	2.6%	17.07%		
Commodities	3.2%	17.69%	Historical Data	
Utilities	3.2%	12.48%	Start:	End:
REITs	3.2%	12.39%	12/31/2003	12/31/2006
Malaysia	3.2%	18.60%	Average Annual Return	Standard Deviation (Annual)
Short-Term Bonds	36.1%	4.93%	10.0%	5.1%
–	0.0%	–		
–	0.0%	–		
–	0.0%	–	Historical Beta: 66.0%	
–	0.0%	–	Historical Yield: 2.0%	
–	0.0%	–	Portfolio R^2: 79.5%	
–	0.0%	–	Performance of S&P 500 over historical period	
–	0.0%	–		
–	0.0%	–	Avg. Ann. Return S&P 500 (no dividends)	
–	0.0%	–	8.4%	
–	0.0%	–	Annual Standard Deviation on S&P 500	
–	0.0%	–	6.9%	
–	0.0%	–		

The risks are the same, but the projected returns are 9.5 percent annually versus 8.7 percent for the Apple Pie version at the same level of risk. Is that a meaningful difference? Look at it this way: In 20 years, with median returns, $10,000 is projected to grow to almost $56,000 with the supercharger but only to about $48,000 without it. The extra $7,000 or $8,000 you stand to collect isn't bad pay for 15 minutes of extra work.

Instead of picking the amount of our bond allocation arbitrarily, we'll do better to plug our portfolio's current value into QPP along with our anticipated future contributions and calculate how much in the way of bonds we really need to hold. This isn't an exact science, but it's probably better than guessing or using some rule of thumb. Moreover, we can check our results over time and make adjustments in the field as needed. Unless we're heirs to a vast fortune, our goal probably will be to fund our retirements successfully while minimizing the stomach-wrenching dips along the way. Monte Carlo studies suggest that a much higher allocation to equities—even as high as 100 percent—can be suitable until we get within a decade of our retirement dates.

Be aware that we haven't "optimized" this portfolio to the *n*th degree. It probably can be improved through further tinkering, at least on paper, but the idea isn't to make a difference out to 16 decimal places. There comes a point (and it comes sooner than you might think) when we're playing with numbers rather than reality. The future is unknown; we're trying to prepare for it as best we can. A Monte Carlo simulator is the best tool currently available in this regard, but it isn't the same thing as getting a future copy of *The Wall Street Journal* a decade early or backdating your stock options.

So that's the basic drill: First, we look at the equity portfolio. Then we pimp the ride with some diversifiers—in this case, using exchange-traded funds—and take it for a spin on the Monte Carlo test track. Finally, we add bonds to reduce the volatility back to where it needs to be.

Lets put some other portfolios through their paces.

The Global Capitalization–Weighted Portfolio with Fries

This portfolio begins with the same weighting as the global capital markets, as shown in Figure 5.5. The components are the same as the Apple Pie portfolio, only the weightings are different, and we've added a 3 percent weighting to Canada. We track it here using the MSCI iShare for Canada, whose ticker is EWC.

Figure 5.5: The GLOB Portfolio

Fund Name	Percentage of Funds	Average Annual Return	Expected Annual Return	Expected Standard Deviation
Total U.S. Stock Market	46.0%	11.10%	11.3%	17.1%
Foreign Developed Market	44.0%	10.51%		
Emerging Markets	7.0%	17.07%		
Canada	3.0%	12.28%	Historical Data	
–	0.0%	–	Start: 12/31/2003	End: 12/31/2006
–	0.0%	–	Average Annual Return	Standard Deviation (Annual)
–	0.0%	–	15.8%	8.7%
–	0.0%	–		
–	0.0%	–	Historical Beta: 113.2%	
–	0.0%	–	Historical Yield: 2.0%	
–	0.0%	–	Portfolio R^2: 80.0%	
–	0.0%	–		
–	0.0%	–	Performance of S&P 500 over historical period	
–	0.0%	–	Avg. Ann. Return S&P 500 (no dividends)	
–	0.0%	–	8.4%	
–	0.0%	–	Annual Standard Deviation on S&P 500	
–	0.0%	–	6.9%	

The baseline portfolio has a projected return of 11.3 percent against a standard deviation of 17.1 percent. We then arbitrarily shrunk the core portfolio down to 84 percent of its original size, to leave 16 percent headroom for the supercharger. This time, instead of using exchange-trades funds as before, we picked 16 individual stocks from Table 4.6.—one for each of the available slots in the QPP tableau. The statistics for our supercharged portfolio are shown in Figure 5.6.

Figure 5.6: The GLOB Portfolio with Fries

Fund Name	Percentage of Funds	Average Annual Return
Total U.S. Stock Market	38.6%	11.10%
Foreign Developed Market	37.0%	10.51%
Emerging Markets	5.9%	17.07%
Canada	2.5%	12.28%
FE	1.0%	15.91%
AFL	1.0%	18.27%
PEP	1.0%	14.73%
FCN	1.0%	36.08%
LMT	1.0%	19.03%
CPK	1.0%	20.68%
SWX	1.0%	14.18%
SO	1.0%	12.67%
NWN	1.0%	9.21%
WGL	1.0%	9.25%
UU	1.0%	17.16%
GIS	1.0%	16.68%
JNJ	1.0%	13.94%
ENB	1.0%	20.58%
MMA	1.0%	16.08%
CLX	1.0%	16.64%

Expected Annual Return	Expected Standard Deviation
12.2%	15.3%

Historical Data

Start: 12/31/2003	End: 12/31/2006
Average Annual Return 15.8%	Standard Deviation (Annual) 7.7%

Historical Beta: 100.3%
Historical Yield: 2.2%
Portfolio R^2: 80.4%

Performance of S&P 500 over historical period
Avg. Ann. Return S&P 500 (no dividends) 8.4%
Annual Standard Deviation on S&P 500 6.9%

The new portfolio has a projected return of 12.2 percent against a standard deviation of 15.3 percent. The reward-to-risk ratio has jumped from 0.66 to 0.80. Why the big improvement? Here's why: The individual stocks had a lower correlation with the initial portfolio than the ETFs we used before did, so adding them resulted in better overall risk-adjusted returns.

Klaxon warning: Unless you're extremely savvy about investing and have the track record to prove it, don't put more than a very small percentage of your money into any one individual company. Don't even start to pick individual stocks until you've sunk the core of your portfolio in broad-based market index funds. This minimizes your individual business risk. One or two percent for an individual stock position seems like a sensible place to be. If someone sues General Mills because their Cheerios got soggy and the stock drops 50 percent, this would limit its impact on your portfolio. Bad things happen to good companies all the time.

Just for kicks, we back tested this portfolio to another time period, the dread March 2000 through March 2003. The generic cap-weighted portfolio had a return of minus 16.9 percent against a standard deviation of 17 percent. What happened to it with our individual stock diversifiers attached? It was down only 10.9 percent against a standard deviation of 14.3 percent. We hope a lightbulb is going off over your head. The best off-the-shelf portfolios that the financial services industry has been peddling are inadequately diversified, and no one even seems to have noticed.

All that remains is to titrate this concoction with bonds to bring it to an appropriate risk level that fits your circumstances. We won't bother with that here because your mileage will vary.

Put It Together

To summarize our process so far:

1. The first step is to enter your current portfolio into a Monte Carlo simulator and note its historical and projected returns and standard deviations.

2. Remove the fixed income holdings. You're going to be using bonds to suppress volatility, not to garner excess returns. You'll add them back in later, as needed.

What's left is just the equity side of our portfolio. Reallocate it proportionally so that these holdings once again total 100 percent, and write down the projected return and standard deviation for the all-equity version. Divide the returns by the risks to get a quick reward-to-risk ratio to facilitate comparison with the variations you'll enter. (These aren't to be confused with the *Goldberg Variations,* which are what Mr. and Mrs. Goldberg tried on their wedding night, according to Woody Allen.)

3. The next step is to study the allocation. The core of the portfolio should broadly access global capital markets, preferably using low-expense, passive index mutual funds or exchange-traded funds. We hope that you see a giant chunk of *one* of the following tickers: SPY, IVV, FSMKX, FSTMX, VFINX, VTSMX, VTI, IWV, TMW, or the like. If not, we recommend a semester at "John Bogle University" for a refresher in Investing 101.

4. What happens next depends on how many holdings you ultimately want to add. If you want to just add a few holdings to set-and-forget your portfolio, plug in the ETFs from Table 4.6 and see how they affect it. We've seen few portfolios that aren't improved by a small allocation to commodities, REITs, and utilities. If yours doesn't already have them, try putting a few percent in each and see how it looks. Then fiddle with adding some others and see if it helps further.

5. If you're willing to go to the trouble of owning individual stocks, then enter the stock tickers from Table 4.6 as a starting point. Include commodities on this list as well, because they have such a low correlation with everything else. You can add REITs and utilities either as a fund or by buying individual securities.

Try to spread the bets around a bit, so that, for example, you aren't just adding a half-dozen bank stocks to the portfolio in the name of diversification. You won't get a big improvement in forward-looking reward to risk if you only add assets that are highly correlated with each other. (The QPP simulator automatically accounts for this in making its calculations).

We don't recommend holding more than 1 or 2 percent of any single company (except Berkshire Hathaway) unless you're an astute investor and have the track record to prove it. You may have to make several passes using QPP to enter the usual suspects from Table 4.6 in order to try them all out against your holdings. Add them to the allocation one by one to see which stocks give you the biggest bang for the buck in terms of increasing your risk-adjust returns (divide the expected returns by the expected standard deviation for a quick measure), and then assemble a team of portfolio diversifiers for your supercharger. It will take some trial and error to see what works best, but it's a more profitable hobby than stamp collecting. For most investors, the goal will be to get the best risk-adjusted expected returns, or the highest return-to-risk ratio.

There's no point in staying up until four in the morning tuning and retuning your portfolio down to the last 100th of a percentage point. If Monte Carlo were an exact forecast of the future, then it would be worth that effort; however, it's not. We see through a glass, darkly. Being approximately right is as well as anyone can do.

6. Once you're satisfied with the look of the portfolio, then add the bonds back until the standard deviation of the entire portfolio equals the standard deviation of the original portfolio in Step 1 of this list. We said to write it down, remember? If your quest has been successful, you won't need to add as much in the way of bonds to get to the same level of volatility. The projected returns of your supercharged portfolio will be improved at the same level of risk.

7. Even better, instead of opting for some arbitrary allocation to bonds, choose the amount that lets you achieve your financial goals while minimizing the volatility along the way. Specifically, we're thinking of the retirement-planning sheets included in QPP, since retirement is the big kahuna of all expenses and the one that will keep you awake at night. Depending on your circumstances, the allocation to bonds will be different from the amount recommended in some portfolio cookbook.

Let's try these steps out with another portfolio.

The Supercharged "Six Ways from Sunday" Portfolio

The Six Ways From Sunday portfolio was the best performer among all the ones we looked at in the last chapter. This portfolio included a giant slug of the two best asset classes over the period we sampled: energy and REITs. It's very hard to improve on this kind of prescience.

Figure 5.7 shows the basic parameters of this portfolio as a starting point.

Figure 5.7: The Six Ways from Sunday Portfolio

Fund Name	Percentage of Funds	Average Annual Return	Expected Annual Return	Expected Standard Deviation
Total Stock Market	16.7%	10.33%	10.0%	10.4%
Total International Market	16.7%	9.91%		
REIT Index	16.7%	11.42%	Historical Data	
Energy Index	16.7%	13.71%	Start: 12/31/2001	End: 12/31/2006
TIPs	16.7%	6.51%	Average Annual Return	Standard Deviation (Annual)
International Bonds	16.7%	8.13%		
–	0.0%	–	14.5%	8.3%
–	0.0%	–		
–	0.0%	–	Historical Beta: 47.3%	
–	0.0%	–	Historical Yield: 3.4%	
–	0.0%	–	Portfolio R^2: 49.7%	
–	0.0%	–		
–	0.0%	–	Performance of S&P500 over historical period	
–	0.0%	–	Avg Ann Return S&P500 (no dividends) 5.0%	
–	0.0%	–		
–	0.0%	–	Annual Standard Deviation on S&P500 12.4%	
–	0.0%	–		
–	0.0%	–		

Note the projected standard deviation of 10.4 percent. This is the figure we're going to try to match with our tweaked portfolio later, so our end portfolio has the same volatility.

We removed the bonds, and now examine the equity side of the portfolio holdings as shown in Figure 5.8.

Figure 5.8: The Six Ways from Sunday Portfolio—Equities Only

Fund Name	Percentage of Funds	Average Annual Return	Expected Annual Return	Expected Standard Deviation
Total Stock Market	25.0%	10.30%	11.3%	15.3%
Total International Mkt.	25.0%	9.91%		
REIT Index	25.0%	11.41%	Historical Data	
Energy Index	25.0%	13.71%	Start:	End:
TIPs	0.0%	6.52%	12/31/2001	12/31/2006
International Bonds	0.0%	8.11%	Average Annual Return	Standard Deviation (Annual)
–	0.0%	–	17.7%	11.7%
–	0.0%	–		
–	0.0%	–	Historical Beta: 76.4%	
–	0.0%	–	Historical Yield: 3.3%	
–	0.0%	–	Portfolio R^2: 65.5%	
–	0.0%	–	Performance of S&P 500 over historical period	
–	0.0%	–		
–	0.0%	–	Avg. Ann. Return S&P 500 (no dividends)	
–	0.0%	–	5.0%	
–	0.0%	–	Annual Standard Deviation on S&P 500	
–	0.0%	–	12.4%	

Next, we removed 20 percent of the equities to make room under the hood for the supercharger. After trial and error, we added 2 percent each of ten stocks from Table 4.6. The resulting portfolio is shown in Figure 5.9.

Figure 5.9: The Supercharged Six Ways from Sunday Portfolio

Fund Name	Percentage of Funds	Average Annual Return	Expected Annual Return	Expected Standard Deviation
Total Stock Market	20.0%	10.33%	11.7%	12.8%
Total International Market	20.0%	9.91%		
REIT Index	20.0%	11.42%	Historical Data	
Energy Index	20.0%	13.71%	Start:	End:
TIPs	0.0%	6.51%	12/31/2001	12/31/2006
International Bonds	0.0%	8.13%	Average Annual Return	Standard Deviation (Annual)
FCN	2.0%	25.93%	16.4%	9.7%
LMT	2.0%	15.53%		
AFL	2.0%	12.19%	Historical Beta: 63.1%	
BUD	2.0%	10.16%	Historical Yield: 2.9%	
JNJ	2.0%	11.32%	Portfolio R^2: 64.2%	
K	2.0%	11.17%		
GIS	2.0%	11.48%	Performance of S&P500 over historical period	
^DJC	2.0%	10.53%	Avg Ann Return S&P500 (no dividends)	
DTE	2.0%	12.21%	5.0%	
NOC	2.0%	13.20%	Annual Standard Deviation on S&P500	
-	0.0%	-	12.4%	
-	0.0%	-		
-	0.0%	-		
-	0.0%	-		

The final step is to add bonds back in to reduce the volatility of the resulting portfolio back to the level of the original in Figure 5.7. The final bond-tempered portfolio is unveiled in Figure 5.10.

Figure 5.10: The Supercharged Six Ways from Sunday Portfolio—Bonds Added Back

Fund Name	Percentage of Funds	Average Annual Return	Expected Annual Return	Expected Standard Deviation
Total Stock Market	16.2%	10.33%	11.1%	10.4%
Total International Market	16.2%	9.91%		
REIT Index	16.2%	11.42%	Historical Data	
Energy Index	16.2%	13.71%	Start:	End:
TIPs	7.6%	6.51%	12/31/2001	12/31/2006
International Bonds	7.6%	8.13%	Average Annual Return	Standard Deviation (Annual)
FCN	2.0%	25.93%		
LMT	2.0%	15.53%	14.9%	8.1%
AFL	2.0%	12.19%		
BUD	2.0%	10.16%		
JNJ	2.0%	11.32%	Historical Beta: 49.8%	
K	2.0%	11.17%	Historical Yield: 3.0%	
GIS	2.0%	11.48%	Portfolio R^2: 57.4%	
^DJC	2.0%	10.53%	Performance of S&P500 over historical period	
DTE	2.0%	12.21%		
NOC	2.0%	13.20%	Avg Ann Return S&P500 (no dividends)	
-	0.0%	-	5.0%	
-	0.0%	-	Annual Standard Deviation on S&P500	
-	0.0%	-	12.4%	
-	0.0%	-		

86

Because the supercharged equity portfolio is less volatile, we need less in the way of bonds to tame it: 15 percent versus 33 percent in the original. In practice, you might want to increase the percentage of bonds slightly beyond this to account for the possibility of increased correlation among portfolio assets going forward. The new portfolio has both bigger historical and expected returns at the same level of risk.

One Lousy Percentage Point— Is That All There Is to Supercharging?

Does a one percentage point increase in annual expected returns really mean anything? Consider the following: Imagine that a 35-year-old woman holding this portfolio wants to retire at age 66. She has $50,000 in savings and is increasing this at an inflation-adjusted $10,000 a year. At this rate, she's set to retire with a median $4.2 million in today's dollars, from which she can draw $75,000 annually and have only a 10 percent chance of going broke by age 90.

What if she held the original, non-souped-up version?

With the same savings at the same rate, her nest egg grows to a median $3.4 million by age 66. This means she can only withdraw $56,000 a year after she retired, with the same 10 percent chance of running out of money by age 90. That's $19,000 less annually that she'll have to spend during her golden years.

Alternatively, she could still reach her retirement goal of $75,000 a year beginning at the age of 66, provided she saves $14,500 in constant dollars every year between now and then—instead of the $10,000 using the supercharged portfolio. That's $4,500 of extra money that has to be salted away year after year.

Here's another way to reach her goal: She can work for an extra three and a half years. That also gives her the 90 percent shot at still being solvent at age 90 while taking out $75,000 a year after retirement.

While she might be up for working all those extra hours, saving all that extra cash, or living on a lot less money, wouldn't it just be easier to invest more intelligently at the front end and let the portfolio do the heavy lifting? That's the difference one measly extra percentage point of returns can make.

Supercharging to Lower Risk

We've been focusing on keeping the risk constant while increasing returns. What about looking at it from the other end—keeping the returns constant while lowering risk? Is this of any real benefit, or does it not matter very much?

This time, the woman has been around the block, so let's put her in the "Four Corners" portfolio—the one that stakes out the four extremes of the U.S. market: small cap, large cap, growth, and value, as laid out in Figure 5.11.

Figure 5.11: The Four Corners Portfolio

Fund Name	Percentage of Funds	Average Annual Return	Expected Annual Return	Expected Standard Deviation
Large Cap Growth	25.0%	10.12%	11.4%	17.2%
Large Cap Value	25.0%	10.74%		
Small Cap Growth	25.0%	12.60%		
Small Cap Value	25.0%	12.15%		
–	0.0%	–	Historical Data	
–	0.0%	–	Start: 12/31/2001	End: 12/31/2006
–	0.0%	–	Average Annual Return	Standard Deviation (Annual)
–	0.0%	–	9.9%	13.3%
–	0.0%	–	Historical Beta: 101.1%	
–	0.0%	–	Historical Yield: 1.0%	
–	0.0%	–	Portfolio R^2: 87.6%	
–	0.0%	–	Performance of S&P 500 over historical period	
–	0.0%	–	Avg. Ann. Return S&P 500 (no dividends)	
–	0.0%	–	5.0%	
–	0.0%	–	Annual Standard Deviation on S&P 500	
–	0.0%	–	12.4%	

This all-equity portfolio is a high risk/high return affair. With this set-up, that 35-year-old woman with $50,000 in her retirement account and who saves an additional $10,000 a year stands to have nearly $4 million in her nest egg the day she retires at the age of 66. Then again, if the markets are less than kind, the 20th percentile of returns would leave her with $2.3 million. (This is an example, not a portfolio recommendation.)

Let's see what happens if we diversify her portfolio using some of the securities in Table 4.6. Our goal is to keep the expected returns constant at 11.4 percent, but to knock the 17.2 percent standard deviation down a peg and see what practical consequences this has.

We trimmed the Four Corners allocation down to 80 percent to make room for the diversifiers. Then we added ten tickers from Table 4.6 and experimented using an equal allocation to each until we found a group that gave us the same expected returns as before. However, due to the greater diversification with lower-volatility stocks, the risks have been lowered, as seen in Figure 5.12.

Figure 5.12: The Four Corners Portfolio Diversified: Same Returns, Lower Risk

Fund Name	Percentage of Funds	Average Annual Return
Large Cap Growth	20.0%	10.12%
Large Cap Value	20.0%	10.74%
Small Cap Growth	20.0%	12.60%
Small Cap Value	20.0%	12.15%
SO	2.0%	10.28%
WM	2.0%	15.47%
BUD	2.0%	10.16%
PEP	2.0%	12.41%
K	2.0%	11.16%
BAC	2.0%	11.24%
NOC	2.0%	13.20%
MMA	2.0%	10.29%
ATO	2.0%	10.57%
JNJ	2.0%	11.32%
-	0.0%	-
-	0.0%	-
-	0.0%	-
-	0.0%	-
-	0.0%	-
-	0.0%	-

Expected Annual Return	Expected Standard Deviation
11.4%	14.9%

Historical Data

Start:	End:
12/31/2001	12/31/2006

Average Annual Return	Standard Deviation (Annual)
10.1%	11.5%

Historical Beta: 86.9%
Historical Yield: 1.5%
Portfolio R^2: 87.5%

Performance of S&P 500 over historical period

Avg. Ann. Return S&P 500 (no dividends)
5.0%

Annual Standard Deviation on S&P 500
12.4%

What does the lower risk do to this woman's retirement plans? With the same savings as before and the same projected returns—but now using a portfolio with a standard deviation of 14.9 percent versus 17.2 percent—her nest egg grows to $4.2 million at retirement versus $4 million using the unsupercharged portfolio. More important, the 20th percentile bad-case nest egg grows from $2.3 million to $2.6 million. Even with a rocky investment future, she ends up with an extra third of a million dollars to spend on herself after she stops working. Or, if she prefers, she can retire a year earlier and be in roughly in the same place financially.

Here's an experiment to try at home: Start a clock today and add up how much work you do in the next year. Now imagine that by a simple portfolio reallocation, you could give yourself all those hours in free time instead. That's the power of lowering risk in this instance.

Summary

To supercharge a portfolio, build an equity core that efficiently siphons earnings from global capital markets, and then add low-correlating assets to diversify it into a high return-to-risk ratio portfolio. Finally, add short-term bonds as required to reduce the portfolio volatility in the service of meeting your investment goals . . . or is there a better way?

Chapter Six

Special Topics:
A Farewell to Bonds?

Using bonds to capture total returns is sending a boy to do a man's job. We add bonds to a capital appreciation portfolio not for the joy of putting money at interest and securing the returns, but in order to have a "safe" investment that won't lose value when the rest of the world comes off the hinges. Could there be a better way of accomplishing the same goal?

Recall that standard deviation measures how far the returns of the security (or a portfolio of securities) are typically dispersed from the mean. A high standard deviation translates into a security or a portfolio that varies more from month to month or year to year than one with a low standard deviation. We tend not to be bothered by stocks that are varying from the mean upward—in fact, we rather like them—but their downward volatility gets our attention fast. Unfortunately, stocks that diverge a lot on the upside are precisely the same ones that do so on the downside.

We *could* just add cash to dampen the raging waters of an equity portfolio, since it has close to zero volatility. Unfortunately, it also has a slightly negative return after inflation. It would be disingenuous to pretend we don't have an eye on returns as well.

Short-term, high-credit-quality bonds fill the bill nicely. They have a mildly positive return and low volatility. Table 6.1 shows how stocks and bonds compare along these dimensions.

Table 6.1: Stocks vs. Bonds 2003–2006		
	Annual Returns	**Standard Deviation**
Stocks (VFINX)	10.1%	6.9%
Bonds (VBISX)	2.4%	1.9%

A quick gander at Table 6.1 suggests what happens when we combine bonds with stocks. The standard deviation falls, but alas, the returns fall as well. This is the price we pay for securing this reduction in volatility. We should note that the period surveyed (2003–2006) was one of exceptionally low volatility for the stock market.

Bonds suppress volatility directly at the expense of our long-term returns, and in so doing increase our even more important risk of running out of money during retirement. That's the trade-off we face.

Is there some method that doesn't involve this hateful compromise between volatility and returns? Can we have our cake (low volatility) and eat the high returns, too?

Our usual method is to use the standard deviation of the target portfolio as the benchmark. Then we supercharge by adding some combination of sectors, countries, and individual stocks. Finally, we pull the dirigible back down to Earth by adding short-term bonds as ballast until the standard deviation of our supercharged portfolio matches the original. The result is higher returns for the same amount of month-to-month risk.

But what if we added more stocks instead of bonds? We've seen that stocks are more volatile than bonds. Some, however, are more variable than others. What if we chose stocks with two special characteristics: low volatility and low-correlation with the rest of our portfolio? We might not be able to do as well as bonds, which are the "killer app" in this regard, but still find something good enough for home use.

Where could an ordinary retail investor find a list of such likely candidates? From Table 6.2, that's where.

Table 6.2: Low Volatility Stocks

Company	Ticker	Business	3-YR. AVG. S.D.
AGL Resources	ATG	Gas Utility	10%
Alleghany	Y	Prop. Insurance	14%
American Express	AXP	Finance	10%
AmeriGas Partners	APU	Oil/Gas	14%
Anheuser-Busch	BUD	Beverages	11%
Atmos Energy	ATO	Natural Gas	12%
Bank of America	BAC	Banking	11%
BB&T	BBT	Banking	14%
BCE	BCE	Telecom	18%
Berkshire Hathaway	BRK-B	Insurance	11%
CH Energy Group	CHG	Electric Utility	12%
Cincinnati Financial	CINF	Prop. Insurance	12%
Clorox	CLX	Household Products	13%
Consolidated Edison	ED	Electric Utility	10%
Diageo	DEO	Beverages	12%
DTE Energy Holdings	DTE	Electric Utility	11%
Erie Indemnity	ERIE	Prop. Insurance	13%
General Dynamics	GD	Aerospace/Defense	10%
Hawaiian Electric	HE	Electric Utility	12%
HSBC Holdings	HBC	Banking	10%
Johnson & Johnson	JNJ	Drugs	10%
Kelloggs	K	Food Manufacturing	9%
Markel	MKL	Prop. Insurance	16%
Municipal Mortgate	MMA	Finance	12%
New Jersey Resources	NJR	Natural Gas	12%
Northrop Grumman	NOC	Aerospace/Defense	12%
Northwest Natural Gas	NWN	Oil/Gas	12%

Table 6.2: Low Volatility Stocks (cont'd.)			
Company	Ticker	Business	3-YR. AVG. S.D.
Peoples Energy	PGL	Natural Gas	17%
PG&E	PCG	Electric Utility	11%
Principal Financial	PFG	Insurance	11%
Progress Energy	PGN	Electric Utility	10%
Progressive	PGR	Insurance	19%
Prudential Financial	PRU	Life Insurance	15%
Sky Financial Group	SKYF	Savings & Loan	18%
Southern Company	SO	Electric Utility	9%
SunTrust Banks	STI	Banking	9%
Swisscom AG	SCM	Telecom	13%
Torchmark	TMK	Life Insurance	10%
United Utilities	UUPLY	Water Utility	13%
Vectren	VVC	Gas Utility	9%
Wal-Mart	WMT	Discount Stores	16%
Washington Federal	WFSL	Savings & Loan	11%
Wells Fargo	WFC	Banking	10%
Wesco	WSC	Insurance	15%
WGL Holdings	WGL	Natural Gas	11%
Wisconsin Energy	WEC	Electric Utility	10%
Wyeth	WYE	Drugs	16%

The usual caveats have to be kept in mind: Any list of stocks selected for some extreme characteristic (for example, low volatility—in this case, their three-year trailing standard deviation) will have a tendency to regress to the mean (toward higher volatility). Also, any list of recommended stocks has a shelf life. You have to do your own due diligence.

Generally speaking, however, we like bigger companies—those that have earnings, that pay dividends (except we like Berkshire Hathaway even though it doesn't pay dividends), that have low price/earnings ratios, and so on. Then, when assembling our shopping list, we like to pick companies from a variety of industries—for example, not ten food-manufacturing companies. But the ultimate test isn't the name of their industry group; it's the intercorrelation of the movements of their stock prices. This is something that QPP's built-in correlation table shows us in an instant.

Something else may strike you about the stocks on Table 6.2. *You've seen many of them before . . . in Table 4.6!* In other words, the same stocks that worked so well to diversify portfolios are the ones that also dampen volatility. This is a major reason why they did such a good job improving risk-adjusted returns.

Since stocks are inherently more volatile than bonds, we'll never equal the bonds' volatility-squashing power. But substituting a portion of our portfolio with low-volatility stocks can often get us to the same place (the same standard deviation), and with higher expected returns.

Figure 6.1 shows a serviceable, if somewhat pedestrian, portfolio consisting of 60 percent S&P 500 index (VFINX) and 40 percent short-term bonds (VBISX).

Figure 6.1: Vanilla 60/40 Portfolio

Fund Name	Percentage of Funds	Average Annual Return	Expected Annual Return	Expected Standard Deviation
S&P 500 Index	60.0%	10.35%	8.2%	9.3%
Short-Term Bonds	40.0%	4.93%		
–	0.0%	–		
–	0.0%	–	Historical Data	
–	0.0%	–	Start:	End:
–	0.0%	–	12/31/2003	12/31/2006
–	0.0%	–	Average Annual Return	Standard Deviation (Annual)
–	0.0%	–	7.0%	4.2%
–	0.0%	–		
–	0.0%	–	Historical Beta: 60.4%	
–	0.0%	–	Historical Yield: 1.9%	
–	0.0%	–	Portfolio R^2: 96.5%	
–	0.0%	–		
–	0.0%	–	Performance of S&P 500 over historical period	
–	0.0%	–	Avg. Ann. Return S&P 500 (no dividends)	
–	0.0%	–	8.4%	
–	0.0%	–	Annual Standard Deviation on S&P 500	
–	0.0%	–	6.9%	
–	0.0%	–		

Note that it has a projected standard deviation of 9.3 percent. This is our target.

Next, we reduce our short-term bond allocation to half of what it was, and then add a chocolate box of low-volatility tickers from Table 6.1. All that remains is to boost our allocation to the low volatility stocks at the expense of the allocation to S&P 500 until we reach the same benchmark standard deviation (9.3 percent) that we have above. It turns out that this requires adding 2.1 percent of each of the 18 securities. We could tweak it for even better numbers, but that might be getting too clever, so we'll just leave them equally weighted. The results are shown in Figure 6.2.

Figure 6.2: Diversifying with Low-Volatility Stocks

Fund Name	Percentage of Funds	Average Annual Return	Expected Annual Return	Expected Standard Deviation
S&P 500 Index	42.2%	10.35%	10.2%	9.3%
Short-Term Bonds	20.0%	4.93%		
HBC	2.1%	7.94%		
NWN	2.1%	9.21%		
PG	2.1%	9.39%		
SO	2.1%	12.68%		
K	2.1%	12.77%		
SCG	2.1%	12.80%		
WEC	2.1%	13.21%		
GD	2.1%	13.41%		
WFC	2.1%	13.44%		
JNJ	2.1%	13.93%		
ED	2.1%	14.06%		
ATG	2.1%	13.31%		
TMK	2.1%	14.13%		
DTE	2.1%	14.22%		
PFS	2.1%	14.35%		
PCG	2.1%	14.26%		
SWX	2.1%	14.18%		
BUD	2.1%	14.91%		

Historical Data

Start:	End:
12/31/2003	12/31/2006

Average Annual Return	Standard Deviation (Annual)
9.3%	4.4%

Historical Beta: 58.4%
Historical Yield: 2.3%
Portfolio R^2: 83.5%

Performance of S&P 500 over historical period

Avg. Ann. Return S&P 500 (no dividends)
8.4%

Annual Standard Deviation on S&P 500
6.9%

Once again, the projected standard deviation has returned to 9.3 percent. How much has this diminution of our S&P 500 holdings hurt us? Not at all. The 60/40 stock/bond portfolio had a historical return of 7 percent and has a projected return of 8.2 percent. Our new portfolio had a historical return of 9.3 percent and has a projected return of 10.2 percent—in other words, our returns look more promising. Bonds are wondrous things, but they can be performance killers. This is the power of low-volatility equities to supercharge your portfolio.

Keep in mind that this solution may end up proposing more than a one percent allocation to each individual stock—purportedly low-volatility stock, to be sure, but certainly with some individual business risk present. We could cut it by buying more and different stocks from Table 6.2. We could also accept a little more individual business risk as a trade-off for the prospect of getting better expected returns.

Objection!

Hold it a minute. We're talking about 2003 through 2006, a happy time for stocks. What about the bad times? Are these stocks really going to be there for us the way our friends the bonds would? These are fair questions. Using the power of QPP, let's go back and sample another time period—the money-annihilating three years following March 2000 (when the Internet/telecom bubble popped). Figure 6.3 shows how the standard 60/40 stock/bond portfolio fared then.

Figure 6.3: Bad Times for the 60/40 Portfolio

Fund Name	Percentage of Funds	Average Annual Return	Expected Annual Return	Expected Standard Deviation
S&P 500 Index	60.0%	10.34%	7.7%	8.8%
Short-Term Bonds	40.0%	3.83%		
HBC	0.0%	12.87%		
NWN	0.0%	10.42%		
PG	0.0%	11.17%		
SO	0.0%	13.67%		
K	0.0%	13.29%		
SCG	0.0%	11.65%		
WEC	0.0%	11.81%		
GD	0.0%	16.51%		
WFC	0.0%	11.88%		
JNJ	0.0%	12.96%		
ED	0.0%	11.18%		
ATG	0.0%	10.08%		
TMK	0.0%	12.58%		
DTE	0.0%	12.41%		
PFS	0.0%	0.0%		
PCG	0.0%	25.02%		
SWX	0.0%	11.06%		
BUD	0.0%	11.04%		

Historical Data

Start:	End:
3/24/2000	3/24/2003

Average Annual Return	Standard Deviation (Annual)
-6.3%	10.3%

Historical Beta: 58.0%
Historical Yield: 2.4%
Portfolio R^2: 99.4%

Performance of S&P 500 over historical period
Avg. Ann. Return S&P 500 (no dividends)
-16.7%
Annual Standard Deviation on S&P 500
17.7%

It isn't pretty. The generic portfolio had a historical annual average return of *minus* 6.3 percent against a standard deviation of 10.3 percent during those times that tried investors' souls. Still, the S&P 500 by itself had an annual average return of minus 15.3 percent during this period.

Okay—so how about the portfolio that used only 20 percent bonds and made up the difference using low-volatility stocks? (One of our 18 companies didn't exist back then, so spread its 2.1 percent share among the remaining 17.) The results are tallied in Figure 6.4.

Figure 6.4: Bad Times for the Low-Volatility Stock Portfolio

Fund Name	Percentage of Funds	Average Annual Return	Expected Annual Return	Expected Standard Deviation
S&P 500 Index	42.6%	10.34%	10.0%	7.2%
Short-Term Bonds	20.0%	3.83%		
HBC	2.2%	12.87%		
NWN	2.2%	10.42%		
PG	2.2%	11.17%		
SO	2.2%	13.67%		
K	2.2%	13.29%		
SCG	2.2%	11.65%		
WEC	2.2%	11.81%		
GD	2.2%	16.51%		
WFC	2.2%	11.88%		
JNJ	2.2%	12.96%		
ED	2.2%	11.18%		
ATG	2.2%	10.08%		
TMK	2.2%	12.58%		
DTE	2.2%	12.41%		
PFS	0.0%	0.0%		
PCG	2.2%	25.02%		
SWX	2.2%	11.06%		
BUD	2.2%	11.04%		

Historical Data

	Start:	End:
	3/24/2000	3/24/2003

Average Annual Return	Standard Deviation (Annual)
0.2%	9.2%

Historical Beta: 45.4%
Historical Yield: 2.6%
Portfolio R^2: 75.5%

Performance of S&P 500 over historical period

Avg. Ann. Return S&P 500 (no dividends)
-16.7%

Annual Standard Deviation on S&P 500
17.7%

This time, the portfolio was down . . . no, wait a minute . . . it was *up* exactly 0.2 percent per year against a standard deviation of 9.2 percent. So instead of losing 6.3 percent a year on average for three years running, we came out . . . ahead? Can you imagine how conceited you would have felt at the time, making money while everyone else was sailing off the edge of the earth? In short, this idea of using stocks to control portfolio volatility appears to have merit.

Figure 6.4 contains another object lesson, this time about the dangers of using recent history to make investment decisions. Look at the difference between the historical performance of this portfolio versus the returns that the QPP Monte Carlo simulator projects for it. Historically, we have a return of 0.2 percent annually and a standard deviation of 9.2 percent. The forward-looking expected returns for the portfolio calculated by QPP were 10 percent against a standard deviation of 7.2 percent. What were the actual returns over the next three years? They were 9.3 percent against a standard deviation of 4.4 percent. The Monte Carlo simulator's internal risk-return balancing saved us from making unrealistic projections.

This is the whole point of using sophisticated statistical tools to analyze and guide our portfolio decisions: to free us from investment myopia. Since investors notoriously abandon today's poor performers in favor of the last year's hottest—only to discover that last year's big news makers are next year's has-beens, this is an important corrective.

Chapter Seven

Special Topics: Roll Your Own Hedge Fund

Over the past ten years, the interest in hedge funds has exploded, in conjunction with the race to build the biggest titanium-headed driver in golf. Part of this is just elitism. Part of it, as Alan Greenspan told Ben's dad (economist Herbert Stein), is the lotto effect: the chance to hit it big.

Over time, however, hedge funds have assembled a track record. Investors have realized that they do not, in aggregate, outperform the S&P 500 index after expenses. Some do, but then we're back to the tiresome game of trying to guess the winning funds in advance.

As a result, hedge funds are increasingly being sold as *alternative* investments rather than *outperforming* investments. They promise to park our money in an investment vehicle that will deliver equity-like returns, but returns that are uncorrelated with the larger stock market, and hence can hedge our stock market investments. The S&P 500 might go down 10 percent one year, but in theory a hedge fund could go up 10 percent that same year. In theory, it's completely uncoupled, so that we have two tickets to win, not just one. On average, three years out of ten, the S&P 500 will lose money. During those three years, the hedge fund will prove especially valuable. (Especially if they work as intended. There are those who think hedge funds are simply a compensation strategy masquerading as an asset class that don't hedge anything. We shall see.) While bonds are a near-perfect hedge, offering low to even a slightly negative correlation with the stock market, we've seen how they leave us swamped in a Sargasso Sea of low returns. Hedge funds, on the other hand, represent an opportunity to lower our overall portfolio risk (by investing partly in a hedge fund and partly in the market) without giving up on returns.

As desirable as owning a hedge fund might sound, you probably either can't have one or don't want one:

- You need to be an accredited investor to apply. That will probably mean $2.5 million in net worth by the time you read this.

- You need to forklift over at least $1 million to get in the door.

- You need to do a great deal of due diligence on the fund. Remember all the ones you read about that turned out to be outright frauds? People lost real money in them, including many smart individuals who thought they'd done enough due diligence. When people say that hedge funds are "lightly regulated," they're not kidding.

- The Groucho effect: You won't want to be a member of any club that will have you as a member. The hot funds you want to join will be closed to new investors, while the ones that will let you in are the ones you don't want.

- You'll have to subject yourself to the fund manager's "black box" investing. Who knows what he's really doing with your money?

- Do you want your money back? You can't have it—at least, right away. You have to write a letter to the fund and then wait a couple of months until the end of the quarter to get it—assuming that all goes well.

- You'll pay a small fortune for the privilege of playing: typically a 2 percent annual management fee, plus 20 percent of all your paper profits.

What are we ordinary investors to do? How about this: Why don't we set up part of our portfolio as a hedge fund in its own right? Let's explore how.

Up until now, we've discussed creating a portfolio and supercharging it by diversifying the core as much as possible. Then we've talked about the possibility of using stocks to lower volatility as a partial bond substitute.

The idea now isn't to optimize the core, as it was previously, but instead to create a parallel universe—a completely new set of holdings with positive expected returns that's as different from the core as possible.

Our technique will be similar to the bond-replacement strategy we discussed in the last chapter, but with this major difference: With the bond-replacement approach, we wanted to find equity investments resembling bonds, whose price movements displayed low volatility (a low standard deviation). With our homegrown hedge fund, we'll be looking for stocks whose price swings are independent from those of the larger stock market. The technical term for this is *low R-squared*.

As we mentioned earlier, the label *R-squared* refers to the extent that a stock's (or, for that matter, a portfolio's) movement is explained by movements in the broader market (with the S&P 500 index acting as the usual benchmark). If a stock has an R-squared of 100 percent, this means that its price fluctuations are perfectly explained by the movement of the S&P 500 as a whole. If it has an R-squared of zero percent, then it moves with complete independence from the stock market.

Note that a stock with a low R-squared can still be quite volatile. A gold-mining stock has returns that don't depend on the price movements of the S&P 500 companies, but can fluctuate wildly depending on the price of gold. So we need to keep in mind that the stocks we're looking for might be very volatile—that's why they aren't bond replacements. However, as along as their returns are proportionate to their risks, and the fortunes are uncorrelated with the S&P 500, we'll consider them.

Where might we find a list of such promising investments for our own private hedge fund? From Table 7.1, naturally.

Table 7.1: Historical R-squared of Selected Stocks

Company	Ticker	Business	2002	2003	2004	2005	2006
AmerisourceBergen	ABC	Medical	1%	5%	29%	22%	0%
Aflac	AFL	Insurance	10%	5%	7%	0%	6%
Apache	APA	Oil & Gas	6%	1%	2%	19%	12%
Ball	BLL	Packaging	0%	1%	23%	18%	20%
BP Prudhoe Bay Royalty Trust	BPT	Oil & Gas	0%	11%	1%	1%	6%
British American Tobacco	BTI	Tobacco	1%	24%	29%	1%	4%
Chesapeake Energy	CHK	Oil & Gas	3%	22%	0%	7%	5%
Chesapeake Utilities	CPK	Gas Utility	3%	24%	2%	3%	1%
City National	CYN	Regional Banks	16%	1%	9%	2%	2%
Dominion Resources	D	Electric Utility	22%	29%	5%	0%	4%
Dress Barn	DBRN	Clothing Stores	13%	7%	11%	6%	8%
DRS Technologies	DRS	Aerospace & Defense	1%	21%	5%	4%	7%
Enbridge Energy LP	EEP	Pipelines	5%	12%	4%	4%	1%
Edison International	EIX	Electric Utility	29%	13%	2%	1%	11%
Endo Pharmaceutical Holdings	ENDP	Drugs	1%	13%	19%	10%	2%
First American	FAF	Title Insurance	9%	15%	13%	24%	6%
First Community Bancorp	FCBP	Savings & Loan	7%	18%	17%	29%	1%
FTI Consulting	FCN	Consulting	12%	1%	0%	3%	18%

Table 7.1: Historical R-squared of Selected Stocks (cont'd.)

Company	Ticker	Business	2002	2003	2004	2005	2006
FirstEnergy	FE	Electric Utility	31%	15%	9%	5%	5%
First Niagara Financial Group	FNFG	Savings & Loan	6%	2%	6%	9%	6%
General Mills	GIS	Food Manufacturing	2%	2%	11%	0%	4%
Orix	IX	Financial Services	33%	0%	12%	4%	10%
Johnson & Johnson	JNJ	Drugs	28%	0%	13%	20%	1%
Lifepoint Hospitals	LPNT	Hospitals	1%	0%	15%	7%	17%
Mine Safety Appliances	MSA	Machinery	5%	1%	1%	21%	1%
Indymac Bancorp	NDE	Savings & Loan	7%	37%	1%	6%	17%
Pacific Capital Bancorp	PCBC	Regional Banks	4%	7%	26%	2%	7%
Public Service Enterprise	PEG	Electric Utility	17%	2%	28%	1%	4%
PPL	PPL	Electric Utility	25%	3%	17%	1%	5%
Ralcorp Holdings	RAH	Food Manufacturing	15%	4%	1%	13%	4%
Renaissance Holdings	RNR	Reinsurance	6%	5%	16%	18%	10%
Constellation Brands	STZ	Beverages	9%	4%	16%	2%	3%
Teppco Partners	TPP	Pipelines	3%	0%	2%	2%	24%
Triad Hospitals	TRI	Hospitals	6%	0%	28%	7%	0%
Umpqua Holdings	UMPQ	Regional Banks	1%	9%	0%	9%	7%
Valero Energy	VLO	Oil & Gas	33%	0%	6%	0%	0%
Wesco	WSC	Insurance	19%	3%	17%	0%	13%

Table 7.1 lists some stocks that have very low R-squared over the recent past (2003–2006). We aren't endorsing any of them, so you'll have to do your own due diligence. This list is a good place to start, but there are undoubtedly many errors of omission and commission.

We came up with our list by starting with a much larger group of companies that displayed a low correlation with the S&P 500 from 2002 to 2006. Then we looked at each company's R-squared for each year over that period, as displayed in the five right-hand columns in Table 7.1. We eliminated companies whose R-squared was too high or too erratic because we were going for consistently low scores.

Then we screened for fundamentals: We eliminated companies who didn't have enough daily trading volume to make them readily liquid, and those who had cut their dividends or whose payout ratios appeared to be unsustainably high. We cut corporations that had no earnings, or whose total returns had declined over the past few years. Finally, we struck those whose price/earnings ratio was more than 25, which meant that they were just too expensive for us to consider. Those that remained are the ones we listed.

Our next step was to assemble some of them into a portfolio. We found that many of these companies had very high standard deviations, so we winnowed these out and tried to pick the least volatile group that also had the lowest R-squared. We also made some effort to select from different industries, including: food, regional banking, insurance, tobacco, a gas utility, medical equipment, packaging, beverages, drugs, and a pipeline limited partnership. Our resulting portfolio is shown in Figure 7.1.

Figure 7.1: Homegrown Hedge Fund

Fund Name	Percentage of Funds	Average Annual Return
General Mills	10.0%	11.48%
Pacific Capital Bancorp	10.0%	16.38%
Wesco	10.0%	10.65%
British American Tobacco	10.0%	14.02%
Chesapeake Utilities	10.0%	12.77%
Amerisourcebergen	10.0%	16.10%
Ball Corporation	10.0%	14.47%
Constellation Brands	10.0%	17.38%
Novartis AG	10.0%	11.10%
Enbridge Energy LP	10.0%	12.27%
-	0.0%	-
-	0.0%	-
-	0.0%	-
-	0.0%	-
-	0.0%	-
-	0.0%	-
-	0.0%	-
-	0.0%	-
-	0.0%	-
-	0.0%	-

	Expected Annual Return	Expected Standard Deviation
	13.6%	9.9%

Historical Data

	Start:	End:
	12/31/2001	12/31/2006

	Average Annual Return	Standard Deviation (Annual)
	15.7%	7.8%

Historical Beta: 19.3%

Historical Yield: 3.3%

Portfolio R^2: 9.3%

Performance of S&P 500 over historical period

Avg. Ann. Return S&P500 (no dividends) 5.0%

Annual Standard Deviation on S&P 500 12.4%

The portfolio's R-squared is 9.3 percent. In other words, its returns are largely disconnected from those of the stock market. Again, to quote from Groucho, "You go Uruguay and I'll go mine." The portfolio itself projects a 13.6 percent in annual expected returns, against a standard deviation of 9.9 percent.

That's probably too optimistic. Even well-designed portfolios have trouble delivering more than a percentage point of return for each percentage point of risk. Furthermore, because these stocks have been selected for their extreme scores on one characteristic (R-squared), it's likely that their R-squared in the future will regress toward the mean (go higher) more than it has in the past.

Should this frighten us? Not necessarily. As long as the portfolio's R-squared remains on the low side and its returns are higher than those from the bond market, this portfolio could provide a worthwhile hedge.

Just for chuckles, we compared the performance of this portfolio with the S&P 500 in an out-of-sample period: the year 2000. This was the beginning of the tech collapse. An S&P 500 index fund was down 8.7 percent that year. What about our homegrown hedge fund? It was up 37.7 percent (and with a lower standard deviation). We doubt that this particular stroke of luck will happen again anytime soon, but it does show a decided lack of correlation to the market as a whole.

What happens when we combine this portfolio with one that's market driven? Figure 7.2 shows a portfolio that's devoted half to the S&P 500 (VFINX) and half to the hedge fund shown in Figure 7.1.

Figure 7.2: Homegrown Hedge Fund + S&P 500

Fund Name	Percentage of Funds	Average Annual Return	Expected Annual Return	Expected Standard Deviation
General Mills	5.0%	11.48%	12.0%	10.0%
Pacific Capital Bancorp	5.0%	16.38%		
Wesco	5.0%	10.65%		
British American Tobacco	5.0%	14.02%		
Chesapeake Utilities	5.0%	12.77%		
Amerisourcebergen	5.0%	16.10%		
Ball Corporation	5.0%	14.47%		
Constellation Brands	5.0%	17.38%		
Novartis AG	5.0%	11.10%		
Enbridge Energy LP	5.0%	12.27%		
S&P 500	50.0%	10.36%		
–	0.0%	–		
–	0.0%	–		
–	0.0%	–		
–	0.0%	–		
–	0.0%	–		
–	0.0%	–		
–	0.0%	–		
–	0.0%	–		
–	0.0%	–		

Historical Data

Start:		End:
12/31/2001		12/31/2006
Average Annual Return		Standard Deviation (Annual)
11.2%		8.3%

Historical Beta: 60.0%
Historical Yield: 2.5%
Portfolio R^2: 80.1%

Performance of S&P 500 over historical period

Avg. Ann. Return S&P 500 (no dividends)
5.0%

Annual Standard Deviation on S&P 500
12.4%

Table 7.2 summarizes the effects of employing different strategies involving different portfolio allocations to the stock market (VFINX), short-term bonds (VBISX), and the little hedge fund we just created.

Table 7.2: Expected Returns and Risks
of Homegrown Hedged Portfolio 2002–2006

Portfolio	Returns	S.D.	Historical R-Squared
100% Bond Index	4.2%	2.8%	8%
100% S&P 500	10.3%	15.2%	100%
100% Homegrown Hedge	13.6%	9.9%	9%
50% Stocks/50% Bonds	7.3%	7.3%	97%
50% Stocks/50% Hedge	12.0%	10.0%	80%

Note again how bonds provide a terrific and reliable hedge, but at the direct expense of performance. An S&P 500 portfolio combined with our homegrown hedge fund offers better returns than the portfolio hedged with bonds, and the result is significantly less dependent on the stock market. We used a 50/50 allocation just to highlight the differences. In reality, we would want to limit the hedge to a much smaller portion of our total portfolio—say, 10 percent (a 1 percent allocation to each stock). We're dealing with individual business risk and need to be careful about holding too great an allocation to a single company that we haven't thoroughly vetted. Just because the hedge might be uncorrelated with the stock market does not mean that it's going to be up when the market is down (the way bonds likely would). It could be down even more.

Still, it illustrates why institutional and high-net-worth investors are so hot to get into hedge funds. If we can't get into their country club, at least we can still swim in our own pool in the backyard. The rich may end up setting soaked anyway.

Chapter Eight

Special Topics:
Investing for Income

One way of deriving income from a portfolio is to invest for capital appreciation and then break off and sell a little piece every so often in order to meet our income requirements. There is, however, another strategy: to invest in income-producing securities and take their payout directly to meet current expenses. Some people (like your authors) use a combination of strategies, investing both for capital appreciation as well as for income. We like income investing well enough to have written a book on the subject: *Yes, You Can Be a Successful Income Investor!* In it, you'll find a broad discussion of income investing options, as well as lists of stocks and REITs that might merit your further investigation. We won't reprint the book here, but will confine ourselves to discussing the overall structure of an income portfolio.

The QPP Monte Carlo simulator has more blades than a Swiss Army knife. One feature we particularly like is that QPP keeps track not only of the historical returns of a portfolio, but also of its historical yield. Up until now, we've been trading off expected total returns against expected risks (standard deviation). Now we'll change the channel and attempt to optimize portfolios for income instead of for total returns. While before we were going after risk-adjusted returns, now we'll seek risk-adjusted yield.

QPP calls the portfolio's yield its "Historical Yield," but strictly speaking, it's really the portfolio's payout ratio. The payout might come from dividends, coupons, capital gains, the sale of options, or even an outright return of principal. QPP doesn't know and, frankly, doesn't care. It's money that the portfolio would have paid out to us over the time frame we sampled.

Another extremely useful piece of data that QPP collects is the "Minimum Rolling 12-Month Yield." A security might have an average yield that's acceptable, but if we're relying on the income from it to put food on the table, we'll also want to look at the lowest payout it made over the period. This gives us a sense of what we might be in for if bad times hit—especially if the period we sampled included any lean times in the first place.

Income portfolios typically include three broad asset classes: bonds, high dividend stocks, and commercial real estate. Let's take them one by one.

Bonds

For capital appreciation portfolios, we've talked about using bonds for their stabilizing influence. For income portfolios, however, we look to bonds for their coupons. A bond is a loan, and the coupons we receive represent the interest on the money we lent. We tend to receive a bigger coupon for making riskier loans or for waiting longer to have them repaid. These bonds are of more interest to income investors than the short-term, high-quality bonds we recommended earlier to suppress volatility in total returns-oriented portfolios. Vanguard's Total Bond Market Index (ticker: VBMFX) is an excellent choice in this regard for tax-deferred accounts, as it captures the returns of the entire U.S. bond market on a capitalization-weighted basis (omitting high-yield or "junk" bonds). iShare's Lehman Aggregate (ticker: AGG) tracks this same index, as does Fidelity's U.S. Bond Index (ticker: FBIDX).

Retirees might want to cut this with an equal measure of inflation-indexed bonds: Vanguard's VIPSX, iShare's TIP, or Fidelity's FINPX. Most of the time these funds provide little diversification from the aggregate bond index above, but if inflation were to hit (and it can arrive unannounced) seniors will be happy to have a meaningful portion of their income portfolios protected against it. Inflation is the great retirement killer.

There are also some other bonds that income investors should at least consider. High-yield bonds, being excluded from the Lehman Bond aggregate, offer the prospect of some diversifying power. Vanguard's High-Yield Bond Fund (VWEHX) is a best-of-breed offering, going after the highest grade of junk bonds (the ones with the least default risk). Be aware that not all high-yield funds are created equal and do your due diligence before buying into this dicey sector. For example, note that Vanguard's fund is often closed to new investors. We urge you to use extreme caution when adding junk bonds. They're called "junk" for a reason: What you gain in yield can quickly evaporate in principal.

Let's toss two more bond sectors into our salad. In this case, we want to sample bonds from outside the United States. On the high-risk side, we have emerging market debt; here we've chosen GMO's Emerging Country Debt fund (GMDFX) as an example. For developed economies, we chose the Delaware Pooled Global Fixed Income fund (DPGIX). These shouldn't be construed as particular recommendations; they're just some five-star funds we picked out of Morningstar's "fund-o-mat" to fill our Monte Carlo's dance card.

We plugged the tickers into QPP and sent it online to gather a few years' worth of data. After adjusting the dials, we decided upon the portfolio shown in Figure 8.1.

Figure 8.1: A Sample Bond Portfolio for Yield

Fund Name	Percentage of Funds	Average Annual Return	Expected Annual Return	Expected Standard Deviation
Total U.S. Bond Mkt.	60.0%	6.42%	7.4%	7.8%
Foreign Bond	20.0%	10.63%		
Emg. Mkt. Bond	10.0%	10.46%		
Hi-Yield Bond	10.0%	4.53%		
-	0.0%	-		
-	0.0%	-		
-	0.0%	-		
-	0.0%	-		
-	0.0%	-		
-	0.0%	-		
-	0.0%	-		
-	0.0%	-		
-	0.0%	-		
-	0.0%	-		
-	0.0%	-		
-	0.0%	-		
-	0.0%	-		
-	0.0%	-		

Historical Data

Start:		End:
12/31/2003		12/31/2006
Average Annual Return		Standard Deviation (Annual)
5.2%		3.6%

Historical Beta: 10.6%
Historical Yield: 5.7%
Portfolio R^2: 4.1%

Performance of S&P 500 over historical period
Avg. Ann. Return S&P 500 (no dividends)
8.4%
Annual Standard Deviation on S&P 500
6.9%

Our portfolio yielded 5.7 percent over the past three years. These asset classes span the world, both geographically as well as in terms of maturity and credit quality.

True confessions: The optimal mix for maximizing the historical yield against the portfolio's projected standard deviation involved a much higher allocation to low-credit quality bonds than made us comfortable. However, we backed away from portfolio optimization greatness in the name of prudence. We wanted the vast majority of the bond portion of our income portfolio to be in investment-grade U.S. bonds (not to be confused with Gary "U.S." Bonds, who danced till a "Quarter to Three").

Our bond allocation ignores taxes. If your bonds are held in a taxable account and you've managed to claw your way out of the lowest tax brackets, you will almost certainly be better advised to use municipal bond funds for a high proportion of your income portfolio. Since pension plans and insurance companies have no use for municipal bonds, they don't buy them and thereby suppress their yields. This means that the yield curve for municipal bonds is usually steeper than it is for taxable bonds, making them a better value for income investors. Vanguard's Intermediate-Term Municipal Income Fund (VWITX) or Fidelity Tax-Free Bond Fund (FTABX) would be a good candidate here; and if you live in a high-tax state, there may be state municipal bond funds that work even better. What will matter most is your after-tax yield. That can include the Alternative Minimum Tax (AMT) as well, so be sure to put that into your hopper. The AMT taxes some types of municipal bonds.

Now that our bond allocation is decided, we can turn to the equity side of our income portfolio.

High-Dividend Stocks

A number of high-dividend exchange-traded funds have launched recently (DVY, PEY, SDY, and the like), making things easy for the dividend-hungry investor . . . and maybe a little too easy. All of these funds have a common issue: In the name of including every possible dividend stock, they achieve a marketlike level of diversification that masks a suboptimal yield.

The performances of many high-dividend stocks are highly correlated with each other, so simply mixing in more and more of them becomes fairly meaningless after a point, in terms of the total diversification benefits it affords. Since there's a finite pool of really high-dividend stocks to begin with, the more we add (50 stocks . . . 100 stocks . . .), the more diluted our dividend yield becomes—the yield that was the only reason we wanted to buy them in the first place. This leaves us with two bad outcomes: a lower-than-desired yield that we don't want, which is purchased at the expense of obtaining a low standard deviation, which we don't need.

Why don't we need the low standard deviation? Because we can always use bonds to decrease the standard deviation of the portfolio without reducing the yield at all.

A better approach, in our view, is to select a small number of high-yielding stocks that are relatively uncorrelated with each other, and look to trade off their yields against their risks. For the years 2003 through 2006, the iShares Dow Jones Dividend Index (ticker: DVY) has had an average dividend yield of 3.3 percent. By way of comparison, Table 8.1 shows a portfolio of ten high-dividend stocks from several sectors, along with their trailing 12-month yields as of this writing.

Table 8.1: Sample Dividend Stock Portfolio Components

Company	Ticker	Sector	Yield
American Capital	ACAS	Business Development	7.2%
Verizon	VZ	Telecom Services	4.3%
Consolitdated Edison	ED	Electric Utility	4.7%
Empire District Electric	EDE	Electric Utility	5.1%
Great Plains Energy	GXP	Electric Utility	5.2%
TrustCo Bank Company	TRST	Regional Bank	6.1%
FirstMerit	FMER	Regional Bank	5.1%
Keyspan	KSE	Natural Gas	4.5%
Nicor	GAS	Natural Gas	4.4%
United Utilities PLC	UUPLY	Water Utility	5.6%

These stocks were selected for their high yields. While there are a lot of utilities, this doesn't really compromise the diversification very much because utility markets are local. We can have undue snow in Denver while it's unseasonably warm in Chicago. Remember that any stock list has a shelf life and may be obsolete by the time you read this.

The portfolio profile that emerges when we put these stocks together is shown in Figure 8.2.

Figure 8.2: Sample High-Dividend Stock Portfolio

Fund Name	Percentage of Funds	Average Annual Return	Expected Annual Return	Expected Standard Deviation
ACAS	10.0%	24.76%	15.5%	19.1%
VZ	10.0%	20.06%		
ED	10.0%	14.06%	Historical Data	
EDE	10.0%	11.79%	Start:	End:
GXP	10.0%	9.89%	12/31/2003	12/31/2006
TRST	10.0%	10.71%	Average Annual Return	Standard Deviation (Annual)
FMER	10.0%	12.96%		
KSE	10.0%	16.13%	11.5%	9.0%
GAS	10.0%	17.92%		
UUPLY	10.0%	17.17%	Historical Beta: 81.2%	
-	0.0%	-	Historical Yield: 5.7%	
-	0.0%	-	Portfolio R^2: 38.6%	
-	0.0%	-	Performance of S&P500 over historical period	
-	0.0%	-	Avg Ann Return S&P500 (no dividends) 8.4%	
-	0.0%	-	Annual Standard Deviation on S&P500 6.9%	
-	0.0%	-		
-	0.0%	-		
-	0.0%	-		
-	0.0%	-		

The projected standard deviation of the portfolio is high at 19.1 percent, but what really matters to us yield-starved income investors is its 5.7 percent historical yield compared with the paltry 3.3 percent we'd have received from the dividend index fund.

The trade-off is that we're taking on more individual business risk. This means we have to do our homework and select our companies with attention to fundamentals. Is their dividend sustainable? Are we paying a reasonable price for the stream of earnings? Are there major risks out there that could torpedo the payout?

We aren't recommending this particular list so much as trying to illustrate a strategy for dividend stock selection. We want to hunt for high-dividend companies with solid fundamentals that we can buy at reasonable prices. Then we want to select stocks that have as low a correlation with each other as possible so that the dividend yield of the portfolio is close to the efficient frontier. We could also cut the risk by adding more individual issues, as long as their yields were still high. In this regard, we have an advantage over the dividend ETFs who are tied to benchmark indexes and their broad mandates. We can custom-tailor our holdings exactly to our personal specifications.

Having selected our high-dividend stocks for our income portfolio, we can proceed to consider real estate investment trusts.

REITs

Throughout this book, we've invoked Cohen & Steers Realty Majors (ticker: ICF) as our default real estate investment trust (REIT) index fund. As successful as ICF has been, it isn't a good choice for income investors because its yield is too low, averaging 3.1 percent over the past three years. Diversification exists to serve some purpose, but what can be an ideal level for the purpose of securing total risk-adjusted returns can be overdiversified for the purpose of getting the highest risk-adjusted yield. That was the case with the dividend stock index fund we just considered, and it's also true with most REIT funds.

Our task will be to select from among only those REITs that pay a high dividend and then use diversification to lower our risk profile as far as possible. Since we're buying individual companies, we also want to consider whether their dividend is sustainable and make sure that we aren't overpaying for the income we're getting. We selected ten such REITs (but of course the list may be outdated by the time you read this), as shown in Table 8.2.

Table 8.2: Sample REIT Portfolio Components

Company	Ticker	Sector	Yield
One Liberty Properties	OLP	Diversified	5.6%
iStar Financial	SFI	Financial	6.2%
United Mobile Homes	UMH	Mobile Homes	6.5%
Hospitality Properties Trust	HPT	Hotels	6.2%
Universal Health Realty	UHT	Healthcare	5.6%
Colonial Properties Trust	CLP	Diversified	5.5%
First Industrial Realty	FR	Industrial	5.7%
National Retail Properties	NNN	Freestanding	5.3%
BRT Realty Trust	BRT	Mortgage	7.3%
Equity One	EQY	Shopping Centers	4.3%

While REITs have become quite expensive lately, we looked for ones with a sustainable payout and a price/earnings ratio under 30. We also wanted them from different sectors where possible. The equal-weighted portfolio they formed is shown in Figure 8.3.

Figure 8.3: Sample REIT Income Portfolio

Fund Name	Percentage of Funds	Average Annual Return	Expected Annual Return	Expected Standard Deviation
OLP	10.0%	14.31%	19.3%	28.3%
SFI	10.0%	14.90%		
UMH	10.0%	16.92%		
HPT	10.0%	12.24%	Historical Data	
UHT	10.0%	30.14%	Start:	End:
CLP	10.0%	22.51%	12/31/2003	12/31/2006
FR	10.0%	25.58%	Average Annual Return	Standard Deviation (Annual)
NNN	10.0%	12.87%		
BRT	10.0%	30.34%	15.2%	14.3%
EQY	10.0%	13.79%		
-	0.0%	-	Historical Beta: 115.9%	
-	0.0%	-	Historical Yield: 6.8%	
-	0.0%	-	Portfolio R^2: 31.3%	
-	0.0%	-		
-	0.0%	-	Performance of S&P 500 over historical period	
-	0.0%	-		
-	0.0%	-	Avg. Ann. Return S&P 500 (no dividends) 8.4%	
-	0.0%	-		
-	0.0%	-	Annual Standard Deviation on S&P 500 6.9%	
-	0.0%	-		

This fund has a historical yield of 6.8 percent and a worst-case historical yield of 5.9 percent. The projected standard deviation is extremely high at 28.3 percent, so it has to be tempered with bonds and the other holdings.

Putting Them All Together

Now that we've assembled an individual portfolio of bonds, stocks, and REITs, how should we combine them in an asset allocation that balances our income requirements against our risk of a loss of principal? Well, the bond portfolio is by far the most efficient at delivering yield per unit of risk. Why not just use bonds for income and forget the rest?

The problem is inflation. The projected growth of the bond portfolio is quite low. If we want our asset base to grow over time—or even keep pace with inflation—we're talking about adding equities (REITs and dividend stocks) to the mix. Otherwise, in real (inflation-adjusted) terms, our income will likely fall. Watch out: Over time, we could suffer a substantial decline in purchasing power.

Currently, all three of our portfolios have roughly the same yield, which hails in the neighborhood of 6 percent. This figure will vary with prevailing interest rates and other factors. The portfolios have different risks. The bonds have a low standard deviation, the dividend stocks have a moderate standard deviation, and the REITs have a high standard deviation. In thinking about how to mix them, we made the simplifying assumption that we'd want to add stocks and REITs to our portfolio in equal measure. Essentially, on the risk-management side, we're back at our familiar game: using equities (stocks and REITs) for growth and bonds for stability.

The critical question becomes: *How much do we want to add in the way of bonds as a stabilizer?* or, to look at it from both sides now, *How much in the way of equities do we want to add in an effort to secure capital appreciation along with our income checks so that our income will keep pace with inflation or even grow over time?* Table 8.3 highlights the expected returns and risks of various combinations of equities and bonds, based on our 2003 through 2006 analysis.

Table 8.3: Expected Rewards and Risks of Income Portfolios						
% Stocks + REITs	100%	80%	60%	40%	20%	0%
% Bonds	0%	20%	40%	60%	80%	100%
Average Yield	6.2%	6.1%	6.0%	5.9%	5.8%	5.7%
Average Total Returns	17.4%	15.3%	13.3%	11.0%	9.4%	7.2%
Standard Deviation	22.9%	19.1%	15.0%	11.8%	9.5%	6.9%
Bad Year	-35%	-29%	-23%	-19%	-15%	-12%

Table 8.3 outlines six possible portfolios, ranging from 100 percent high-dividend stocks and REITs (half and half) with no bonds on the left side to a portfolio of no equities or real estate but consisting of 100 percent bonds on the right side, stepping across in 20 percent increments. On the top line, we note that the yield from these income portfolios is similar. But along their second and third lines, we see that their returns and risks go down dramatically as we add bonds. Finally, the last line shows how much such a portfolio might fall in a really bad year after we pull out our yield.

Note that while this example combines dividend stocks and REITs in equal numbers, a better way to go might be to combine individual stocks and REITs according to which companies offered the best histori-cal yield-to-standard-deviation ratio, without worrying about whether you had an even number of each type.

Figure 8.4 plots this same data on a chart to show the reward-to-risk trade-offs after the income investors have pulled their annual draws from each of these portfolios.

Figure 8.4: Rewards and Risks of Income Portfolios

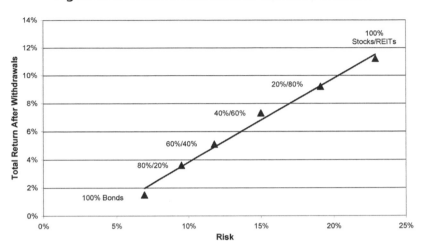

Dealing with Inflation

What jumps out at us is that the 100 percent bond investors are going to lose money over time because their portfolio growth rate of about 1.5 percent after withdrawals is less than the average rate of inflation. While their income stream should be reasonably stable, they face the near-certain prospect of declining purchasing power over time.

The 80 percent bond/20 percent equity investors have a growth rate of about 3.7 percent after withdrawing their annual yield. This is competitive with historical rates of inflation, which have hovered between 3 and 4 percent over long periods. Their net asset values will fluctuate more, as their portfolios rise and fall with market conditions. This is the price they have to pay to obtain the growth required to keep their purchasing power constant.

The 60 percent bond/40 percent equity investors have a post-withdrawal projected growth rate of more than 6 percent—very comfortably above the long-term rate of inflation. If all goes well, their purchasing power should grow over time. The trade-off is that more of the net asset values of their portfolios are exposed to the greater vicissitudes of the equity markets. The income stream should be reliable, though, as the coupons and dividends and rents continue to be passed through to the owners of the income securities.

Since income investors are often retirees, a lingering question is to what extent the Consumer Price Index (CPI) will reflect their experience of inflation. It could be that the specialized goods and services that retirees consume (for example, health care that isn't otherwise covered by Medicare) will become increasingly burdensome relative to the reported CPI, which in the end is a "managed" figure with "hedonic" adjustments—and which is susceptible in the worst case to political manipulation. It might be wise to err on the side of having slightly too much in the way of equities rather than too little.

Beyond the Goldilocks 20 to 40 percent equity mark, income investors are really opting for growth and taking unnecessary risks if their goal is only to secure an income stream that maintains purchasing power over time. They might be better advised to consider a capital appreciation/total returns investment strategy to meet their goals or, barring that, to save money paid out during the good years to supplement their incomes during the bad.

There are many other aspects to income investing that we haven't considered here, such as dividend timing (as practiced by ADVDX, the Alpine Dynamic Dividend Fund), the use of options (as practiced by covered call funds), and especially the addition of leverage—the secret sauce behind many of the closed-end fund offerings. Once we have a diversified portfolio of income securities that give us a high risk-adjusted yield, we can add these like curry powder to give our payout a little extra zing, if they otherwise make sense.

The larger point is that investing for capital appreciation isn't the only game in town. If you're retired or otherwise living off your savings, investing for income has a legitimate role in your portfolio, and Monte Carlo simulation can help optimize the amount of yield you receive for the amount of risk you take. Income strategies go together with growth strategies like Lennon and McCartney when you're 64.

Chapter Nine

Step 6: Do a Portfolio Reality Check

Before you lay down your money, it's important to step back and do a portfolio reality check. Monte Carlo simulation is the best tool available today to analyze a portfolio's prospective performance, but like any tool, it can be dangerous if used ineptly. In this chapter, we'll talk about some things to watch out for.

We'd be remiss if we failed point out that the most brilliant Monte Carlo analysis of your holdings won't help you one bit if you're otherwise making beginner investment bloopers. Rookie mistakes will do you far more damage than having a supercharged portfolio will do you good.

First on our list would be to make sure that the rest of your financial life is in order. There's little point endlessly diddling the dials on your $10,000 savings when you have $30,000 of revolving debt on your credit cards. Don't worry about managing your 100 shares of Yahoo! if you don't have a steady job.

For example and pointedly, most Americans are woefully undersaving for retirement. A sizzling asset allocation isn't going to help them if they're not putting enough away. A person who saves regularly and parks his money in a lowly, one-star-rated Morningstar stock fund is going to be a lot better off than someone with a passel of five-star funds but no money in his account.

The next great enemy of investment returns is hyperactivity. Many people become investment junkies who use buying and selling stocks as a form of self-stimulation. They're likely to be swayed by pronouncements from Wall Street wizards, newsletters, headlines, and yesterday's hot performers, and constantly hop from one bandwagon to the next in their search for the ultimate. Almost invariably, they're led to buy in the euphoria as the market tops and then sell in panic at the bottom. Every study shows that these people underperform the market averages. If you're constantly getting hot and cold feet, 'tis a far, far better thing that you simply buy an index fund and stay the course while finding a new hobby.

The next thing is to pay close attention to fees and expenses. Investing has costs that subtract directly from your returns. That's basic arithmetic. The financial services industry naturally wants to play as big a role as possible in your life and maximize its share of the pie. Many people have little interest or ability in managing their own money, and for them, this level of service is quite appropriate and necessary. On the other hand, if you're sufficiently informed and motivated, you can do a lot of the work yourself and save a bundle by minimizing the role of financial intermediaries. You'll be vigilant in searching out low-expense index mutual funds and low-expense trading platforms and pursuing tax-efficient strategies.

The subject of fees and expenses brings up another important point: Small differences grow to become big ones over time. As we've seen, an investment strategy that offers you fractionally better returns for the same risk—or, for that matter, slightly less risk for the same returns—can be extremely important to your long-term net worth—especially if the rest of your financial life is sufficiently organized to benefit from it.

Monte Carlo Mistakes

The continual temptation is to overtune a portfolio to fit the unique historical data upon which it's predicated. It's always possible, with the aid of hindsight, to concoct portfolios that demolish the benchmarks and deliver outstanding returns with trivial risks. Investing, however, isn't so easy. The portfolio that fits the historical record like a jacket and trousers from a Savile Row tailor falls apart like a cheap suit when it meets the unexpected contingencies of the future. The failure of

Long-Term Capital Management, the hedge fund marketed by Nobel-prize winners that nearly took down the global capital markets, is the relevant morality play for our time in this regard.

Your goal should be modest: getting a reward that's roughly equal to your risk, a projected return that's in line with your portfolio's projected standard deviation. Tuning your portfolio much past this point isn't likely to be highly productive because you'll be tuning the model to the specifications of the internal algorithms of the Monte Carlo simulator, not to the fickle fortunes of the future.

When QPP samples securities whose returns are far outside the norm, there's likely to be a greater margin of error in its projections than when it imports a data series that lies closer to the conventional reward/risk line on Table 3.1 (see page 23). The risk is that it may not bring the latest high flyer down far enough.

There are several ways to deal with this contingency. One is to override the projections and dial back the projected returns further—say, to a market level of return—then see if the portfolio still makes sense. Another fix is to sample data from a different time period—one when our recent high flyer wasn't flying so high—and see how the portfolio works at that point. Our goal should be to build a well-constructed portfolio that can suffer the slings and arrows of market forces in a variety of situations and emerge intact from the ordeal.

Does It Make Sense?

The Monte Carlo simulator knows nothing of the inputs you give it beyond the historical data that it samples. It might be that you hit upon a fortuitous combination of silver age Green Lantern comic books, Miami condominiums, South African diamond stocks, and Château Margaux futures that promise stratospheric returns against trivial risks. Should you take the plunge?

Of course not! This is a patent misuse of the technology. While you might have hit upon the investment idea of the century, there's also the very lively possibility that you have uncovered a specious statistical concatenation that will unravel and take you and your money with it. If your overall portfolio doesn't broadly access the returns of global capital markets, you're proceeding down a road less traveled that may not take you where you want to go. If you can't see a convincing rationale why your portfolio makes sense, don't do it.

As we stated in *Yes, You Can Time the Market!:* "Do not invest in things you do not understand; do not put a penny in a gumball machine unless you can see a gumball inside the machine." Common sense should prevail at all times. Don't use the Monte Carlo simulator as a "black box" financial supercomputer to justify any investment choice that doesn't otherwise make good sense to you.

Split the Difference

Here's a piece of sound advice about how to handle a portfolio. *When in doubt, split the difference.* If you have two good investment ideas and can't decide between them, the best approach is often to divide your allocations between each strategy. It's more important to be half right than to risk being completely wrong. The diversified investor is always in the position of wishing he owned more of the big winners and fewer of the big losers—we all want to be the one with only the milk and none of the duds.

Unfortunately, trying to become that person seems to make *us* big losers. It makes us prey to investment strategies that appeal to immature personalities who want something for nothing or who are looking to get rich quick. To be a diversified investor is to be the sadder-but-wiser girl who accepts (indeed, embraces) compromise as the inevitable price for securing above-average, long-term, risk-adjusted returns. You won't find this gal bragging by the watercooler; instead, she's quietly working at her desk.

Portfolio Rebalancing

The financial services industry loves to tout portfolio rebalancing as a value-adding strategy. The idea is that every year we should sell a little of that 12 months' winners and use them to buy the current losers so that we bring our portfolios back into alignment with their original specs. Thus, if we had a portfolio of 60 percent stocks and 40 percent bonds initially, and at the end of the year find ourselves with 62 percent stocks and 38 percent bonds, we'd sell the extra 2 percent from the stock side and add it to the bond side. Although it can incur tax and transaction costs, rebalancing is promoted on the idea that it gets us into a righteous "sell high, buy low" discipline.

Most of the studies we've read on the topic are either theory based or derived from simple 60/40 stock/bond portfolios drawn from the historical record. This greatly oversimplifies an important question. We looked at 10,000 Monte Carlo simulations involving complex, seven-asset-class portfolios. We experimented with several calendar-based strategies, rebalancing the portfolios monthly, annually, or never. We also looked at some tolerance-based approaches: rebalancing when the portfolio wandered 10, 15, and 20 percent from its original allocations. (Your authors are grateful to Chartered Financial Analyst Bill Swerbenski for modifying his Portfolio Survival Simulator to enable us to make these calculations.) The results of these different approaches are all shown in Figure 9.1.

Figure 9.1: Returns and Risks of Different Portfolio Rebalancing Strategies

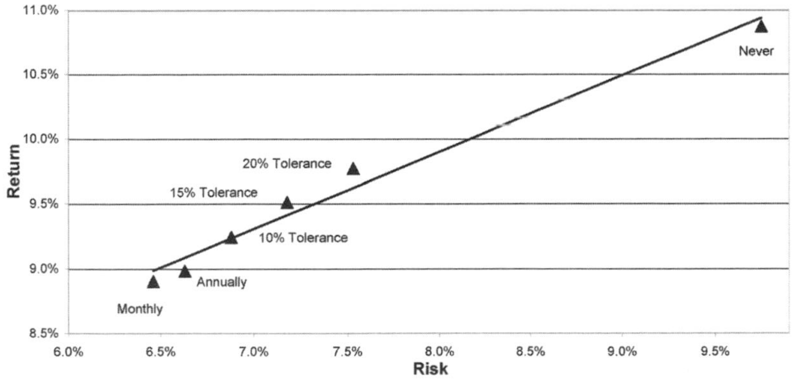

Each triangle in Figure 9.1 represents a specific rebalancing strategy and its effects on the 10,000 portfolios' returns and risks. Note especially the "line of best fit" that indicates the average trade-off between risk and return of all these approaches.

The first thing that stands out is that the more frequently we rebalance, the worse our returns. The next obvious element is that, as is commonly observed, rebalancing cuts our risks. What we'd hasten to add, however, is that it doesn't cut our risks *efficiently.* Specifically, the most frequently recommended ritual—annual realignment—puts our portfolio's returns-to-risk profile below the efficient frontier.

Tolerance-based approaches, on the other hand, seem to have more merit: Those portfolios that were allowed some leeway to roam before being rebalanced had better risk-adjusted returns (above the line) than those adjusted according to the calendar (below the line).

This shouldn't be surprising. Rebalancing pits two well-documented market effects against each other: momentum versus valuation. The problem is, momentum often wins in the short run. When we rebalance frequently, it just shuffles short-term market noise into our portfolios. But rebalancing only when market action has had a chance to push our portfolios significantly out of alignment allows us to take advantage of both market momentum and misvaluation effects that aren't otherwise captured by asset-allocation strategies.

When the costs of rebalancing are pointed out, advocates argue that it's really being done to control risk. This may be true, if the only risk we're talking about is standard deviation. But what about the danger of running out of money? Figure 9.2 shows how, starting with $1,000 invested across seven asset classes, the worst 5th percentile portfolio out of 10,000 grew after 25 years in the markets when following each of these rebalancing strategies.

Figure 9.2: Long-Term Growth
of $1,000 Under Different Rebalancing Strategies

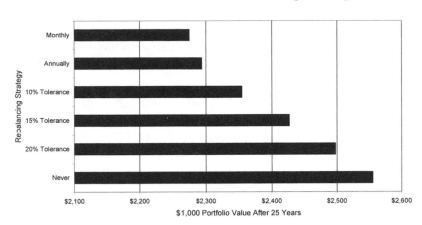

Even in the bad-case scenario, overactive realignment costs us money if we're long-term investors. We can supercharge our long-term returns by not rebalancing our holdings too often.

What If the Supercharger Is Better Than the Engine?

The supercharger all by itself can be a better portfolio than the engine. We saw that this was the case with both our low volatility and hedge fund stocks. We tremble to suggest it, but it is at least a possibility that the market presently fails to value these companies sufficiently for their potential contribution to a portfolio. If the engine is the indexed GLOB portfolio, do we want to junk it for the sake of our 10 or 20 hand-picked stocks? This depends first of all on our tolerance for tracking error—our willingness to experience results different from the market as a whole. If we're institutional investors whose feet are held to the fire every quarter, our tolerance for this sort of outcome is likely to be small. But if we're managing our own money, we might be willing to be the kid who's doing his own thing while the other kids are all doing the same.

Your authors think that the model of using broad-based index funds for the portfolio engine, supercharged with sector ETFs and some individual stocks, is the preferred way to go for most investors.

Individual Stocks

Throughout this book, we've had occasion to point out how the judicious selection of individual stocks can have a beneficial effect on a portfolio's return/risk characteristics. *In effect, we've now come full circle: from the GLOM portfolio of individual cats and dogs . . . to the more efficient GLOB portfolio indexing global markets . . . to the Supercharged GLOB portfolio with various sectors, countries, and individual stocks added . . . all the way back to a portfolio built entirely of individual stocks, this time selected for their special contributions to a portfolio.* This is for advanced students only.

Let us qualify this by passing along a piece of advice from Warren Buffett: Don't buy stocks; buy companies. When you buy a stock, remember that you're buying an organization, not a pretty certificate— not a name, an idea, or a "pick." Don't buy stock in any corporation that you wouldn't otherwise want to own. Make sure it's a business that you'd want to have in its own right.

There have been numerous tomes written on evaluating individual companies, so we won't regurgitate that here. You'll want to look for operations whose stock is liquid, that have a history of earnings growth, that pay a steady and increasing dividend, that have some competitive advantage in a field where there are significant barriers to entry, and whose stock is selling for a reasonable multiple of earnings for its industry group. If you're unfamiliar with individual stock selection, a careful reading of the annual letters of Warren Buffett and the writings of Charlie Munger will quickly set your thinking cap on straight. Monte Carlo analysis might suggest that many stocks are salubrious for a portfolio, but don't buy them unless they're good businesses in their own right and selling at a reasonable price.

Most investors radically overestimate their competence in this area. They think that by reading a newsletter they can take money from the army of finance MBAs on Wall Street who spend 18 hours a day studying the market. Here's a quick test: How much money did you make by stock picking from March 2000 through March 2003? If you did a good job then, you might consider pursuing a portfolio of individual stocks.

If you find yourself beating the market year after year on a risk-adjusted basis, then you surely don't need our permission to proceed—

you're already doing it. If you have some doubts, if you're not sure how an honest accounting of your track record would hold up versus the relevant indexes, then why not make the incredibly smart move to index your core holdings. Know your limitations; you don't have to be a genius at everything. If you do nothing more than move your holdings to the Margarita Portfolio (see page 43), you probably will have gotten more than your money's worth from this book.

If we were going to build a portfolio of individual stocks, we'd want to start with global dominating companies—giants that are almost like mutual funds unto themselves, with worldwide brands, products, markets, and distribution. We screened for businesses larger than $10 billion in market capitalization, and then—since risk is ever the problem with individual stocks—selected the 20 with the lowest standard deviations. We list them in Table 9.1, and you'll find that you've probably heard of some of these.

Table 9.1: Low Volatility Global Dominating Stocks 2002–2006		
Company	Ticker	Industry
Bank of America	BAC	Banking
Berkshire Hathaway	BRK-B	Insurance
Chevron	CVX	Oil
Coca-Cola	KO	Beverage
ExxonMobil	XOM	Oil
General Electric	GE	Electric & Industrial
GlaxoSmithKline Beckman	GSK	Electric Utility
HSBC Holdings	HBC	Banking
Johnson & Johnson	JNJ	Drugs
Nestle	NSRGY	Food Manufacturing
Novartis ADR	NVS	Drugs
PepsiCo	PEP	Beverage
Petróleo Brasileiro ADR	PBR	Oil
Pfizer	PFE	Drugs
Proctor & Gamble	PG	Personal Products
Total SA ADR	TOT	Oil
Toyota	TM	Automobile
UBS AG	UBS	Finance
Wal-Mart	WMT	Discount Stores
Wells Fargo	WFC	Banking

Since we didn't want our portfolio to be redundant, we winnowed the list further by picking the one stock from within each industry group that had the lowest standard deviation. For example, instead of owning Chevron, ExxonMobil, Petróleo Brasileiro, and Total SA, we just picked Total SA. This left us with the distilled giant ten-stock, low-volatility portfolio shown in Table 9.2.

Table 9.2: Distilled Low Volatility Global Dominating Stocks

Company	Ticker	Industry
Berkshire Hathaway	BRK-B	Insurance
General Electric	GE	Electric & Industrial
Nestle	NSRGY	Food Manufacturing
Novartis ADR	NVS	Drugs
PepsiCo	PEP	Beverage
Proctor & Gamble	PG	Personal Products
Total SA ADR	TOT	Oil
Toyota	TM	Automobile
Wal-Mart	WMT	Discount Stores
Wells Fargo	WFC	Banking

This is not a bad portfolio all by itself. We thought to supercharge it by adding some of the individual stocks we'd considered before. Our hope was to do double duty with our selections, so we linked together our previous lists with the stocks that looked the most interesting. These are shown in Table 9.3. Remember that all these lists are just starting points, and we don't pretend that they're by any means complete.

Table 9.3: Cross-Referenced Stocks

Company	Ticker	Industry	Dominator	Diversifier	Low SD	Low R^2
Anheiser-Busch	BUD	Beverage		X	X	
Bank of America	BAC	Banking	X		X	
BCE	BCE	Telecom		X	X	
Berkshire Hathaway	BRK-B	Insurance	X		X	
Chesapeake Utilities	CPK	Gas Utility		X		X
Clorox	CLX	Household Products		X	X	
Consolidated Edison	ED	Electric Utility		X	X	
DTE Energy Holdings	DTE	Electric Utility		X	X	
FirstEnergy	FE	Electric Utility		X		X
FTI Consulting	FTI	Consulting		X		X
General Mills	GIS	Food Manufacturing		X		X
HSBC Holdings	HBC	Banking	X		X	
Johnson & Johnson	JNJ	Drugs	X	X	X	X
Kellogg	K	Food Manufacturing		X	X	
Municipal Mortgage	MMA	Finance		X	X	

Table 9.3: Cross-Referenced Stocks (cont'd.)

Company	Ticker	Industry	Dominator	Diversifier	Low SD	Low R^2
New Jersey Resources	NJR	Gas Utility		X	X	
Northrop Grumman	NOC	Aerospace/Defense		X	X	
Northwest Natural Gas	NWN	Oil & Gas		X	X	
Novartis ADR	NVS	Drugs	X	X	X	X
PepsiCo	PEP	Beverage	X	X		
Proctor & Gamble	PG	Personal Products	X	X		
Public Service Enterprises	PEG	Electric Utility		X		X
Southern Company	SO	Electric Utility		X	X	
United Utilities	UUPLY	Water Utility		X	X	
Valero Energy	VLO	Oil & Gas		X		X
Wal-Mart	WMT	Discount Stores	X		X	
Wells Fargo	WFC	Banking	X		X	
Wesco	WSC	Insurance			X	X
WGL Holdings	WGL	Gas Utility		X	X	
Wyeth	WYE	Drugs		X	X	
Wyeth	WYE	Drugs		X	X	

We also didn't want to duplicate the companies that were on our original list. The ones we chose to add were primarily utilities, to further reduce volatility. The final portfolio of individual stocks we settled on is shown in Table 9.4.

Table 9.4: Sample Portfolio of Individual Stocks		
Company	**Ticker**	**Industry**
Berkshire Hathaway	BRK-B	Insurance
Chesapeake Utilities	CPK	Gas Utility
DTE Energy Holdings	DTE	Electric Utility
FirstEnergy	FE	Electric Utility
FTI Consulting	FTI	Consulting
General Electric	GE	Electric & Industrial
General Mills	GIS	Food Manufacturing
Nestle	NSRGY	Food Manufacturing
Northrop Grumman	NOC	Aerospace/Defense
Novartis ADR	NVS	Drugs
PepsiCo	PEP	Beverage
Proctor & Gamble	PG	Personal Products
Southern Company	SO	Electric Utility
Total SA ADR	TOT	Oil
Toyota	TM	Automobile
United Utilities	UUPLY	Water Utility
Wal-Mart	WMT	Discount Stores
Wells Fargo	WFC	Banking
WGL Holdings	WGL	Gas Utility
Wyeth	WYE	Drugs

The Monte Carlo simulation of this 20-stock portfolio—composed of 80 percent global titans and 20 percent diversifiers—is shown in Figure 9.3. It's gleaned from the most recent five years of data.

Figure 9.3: Sample Portfolio of Individual Stocks

Fund Name	Percentage of Funds	Average Annual Return	Expected Annual Return	Expected Standard Deviation
Berkshire Hathaway	8.0%	10.88%	12.4%	10.3%
General Electric	8.0%	14.57%		
Nestle	8.0%	11.07%		
Novartis	8.0%	11.10%	Historical Data	
PepsiCo	8.0%	12.41%	Start: 12/31/2001	End: 12/31/2006
Proctor & Gamble	8.0%	10.28%		
Total SA ADR	8.0%	13.32%	Average Annual Return	Standard Deviation (Annual)
Toyota	8.0%	15.09%		
Wal-Mart	8.0%	13.71%	11.4%	7.0%
Wells Fargo	8.0%	10.07%		
Chesapeake Utilities	2.0%	12.76%	Historical Beta: 43.5%	
DTE Energy Holdings	2.0%	12.21%	Historical Yield: 2.1%	
FirstEnergy	2.0%	13.75%	Portfolio R^2: 58.2%	
FTI Consulting	2.0%	20.48%	Performance of S&P500 over historical period	
General Mills	2.0%	11.48%		
Northrop Grumman	2.0%	13.20%	Avg Ann Return S&P500 (no dividends)	
Southern Company	2.0%	10.30%	5.0%	
United Utilities	2.0%	11.80%	Annual Standard Deviation on S&P500	
WGL Holdings	2.0%	9.96%	12.4%	
Wyeth	2.0%	18.23%		

This portfolio has an expected return that's higher than its standard deviation. Anything much over a projected future one-to-one ratio makes us suspicious. Maybe this is compensation for individual business risk, or maybe there's risk in the portfolio that isn't captured by standard deviation. Even so, it looks like a reasonable set of holdings. The ten giants give us an anchor of the global marketplace, and the other companies should provide some diversification. While we'll certainly ride with the markets, this isn't a balloon of tech stocks that's going to blow up in our faces. So we'll take the expected mean and standard deviation as approximations: Even if our returns don't turn out to be as great as we hope, and the volatility regresses upward toward the mean, we'll still expect to see our risks and returns in some kind of rough balance. For an all-equity portfolio, this is one that will let us sleep at night.

We hasten to add once again that we aren't recommending that you go out and buy this portfolio. We're only showing one way that an all-individual-stock set of holdings might be assembled to provide a reasonable degree of safety. There are undoubtedly far better ways of doing it.

The End

Dear reader, we hope to have shown you how to make your portfolios work harder for you. As Freud said to Jung, "Learn, and earn."

Appendix A

Berkshire Hathaway by Way of Monte Carlo

Berkshire Hathaway (BRK) is the holding company run by the world-famous genius investors Warren Buffett and Charlie Munger. Buffett took over the company in 1963; at the time, the stock was selling for $18 a share. Today it sells for more than $100,000 a share, and many people feel it's underpriced.

Berkshire Hathaway now holds a number of individual companies (around 80), and more than that if you count their various subsidiaries. These organizations fall into four broad areas: insurance; utilities; finance; and a fourth domain they call "manufacturing, services, and retail." In addition, it holds a lot of cash, not due to the love of cash so much as the absence of current good investing opportunities. While Buffett and Munger prefer to buy companies outright (for tax reasons), they also own a large stock portfolio of publicly traded companies.

Just for fun, we attempted to cram Berkshire Hathaway's top holdings in the Monte Carlo simulator. Since most of these holdings aren't publicly traded, we had to make some judicious substitutions. For example, about 27 percent of Berkshire Hathaway is in the insurance business, with the privately held General Re and Geico being the prime movers. To match these, we substituted four publicly traded insurance companies as a proxy: AIG, Allianz, State Farm, and Progressive. No doubt Buffett and Munger wouldn't be so nonchalant about making substitutions, but we aren't trying to clone BRK so much as to understand the structure of its portfolio.

For their utilities, we used IDU, the S&P utility sector fund. For finance, we substituted XLF, the S&P financial sector fund. For cash, we chose an ultra-short bond fund (SIGVX). We used the Retail HLDRs fund (RTH) for "retail."

Then it got trickier. We decided on Fidelity's Select Industrials sector fund (FCYIX) for "manufacturing"; and having plum run out of ideas, we used Walgreens and McDonald's to cover the "services" part. Hey—if we could pick stocks like Warren and Charlie, we'd be retired in Tahiti instead of writing this book. Finally, we entered some of the biggest holdings from Berkshire's stock portfolio, and substituted IJJ (the iShares Mid-cap Value ETF) for the smaller fry.

The resulting portfolio is shown in Figure A.1. Remember, this isn't an attempt to replicate BRK so much as a Frankenstein monster of it created from parts dug up at the graveyard. If you want BRK, please buy the real thing.

Figure A.1: Simulated Berkshire Hathaway

Fund Name	Percentage of Funds	Average Annual Return	Expected Annual Return	Expected Standard Deviation
AIG	10.0%	11.81%	12.7%	13.3%
AZ	10.0%	20.32%		
ALL	3.6%	17.60%		
PGR	3.6%	22.95%	Historical Data	
IDU	5.6%	12.48%	Start:	End:
XLF	4.5%	9.10%	12/31/2003	12/31/2006
FCYIX	5.1%	12.59%	Average Annual Return	Standard Deviation (Annual)
MCD	2.5%	14.25%		
WAG	2.5%	22.67%	9.6%	6.0%
RTH	5.0%	10.34%		
SIGVX	21.4%	3.70%	Historical Beta: 79.1%	
KO	4.7%	17.67%	Historical Yield: 1.4%	
AXP	4.6%	10.36%	Portfolio R^2: 81.6%	
WFC	3.5%	13.44%	Performance of S&P 500 over historical period	
PGR	3.2%	22.95%		
MCO	1.7%	24.72%	Avg. Ann. Return S&P 500 (no dividends)	
WSC	1.4%	18.49%	8.4%	
BUD	1.0%	14.91%	Annual Standard Deviation on S&P 500	
JNJ	1.0%	13.93%	6.9%	
IJJ	5.0%	12.94%		

What jumps out is that despite Buffett's and Munger's folksy image—the sort who can't relate to the "ivory tower" Modern Portfolio Theory gang and who sit around the cracker barrel playing checkers all day until the phone rings and someone offers them a good company to buy—they've assembled an astonishingly well-diversified set of holdings. Their portfolio has greater historical returns than the stock market as a whole, with less risk. It mixes highly volatile stocks with low-volatility stocks. Its individual holdings don't march to the drum of the stock market, and in addition have a low degree of correlation with each other.

Warren Buffett doesn't have a computer in his office. We suppose that if you have a Monte Carlo chip built into your brain, you don't really need one on your desk. This isn't an idle simile: The distribution of risk inherent to Buffett's managing of Berkshire's "big catastrophe" insurance policies involves the precisely same skill set as distributing risk among a group of investments.

Geoff Considine did a similar analysis looking only at Berkshire Hathaway's publicly traded stock portfolio, with highly similar findings. His paper is available at the Quantext Website (**www.quantext. com**).

The question we posed earlier—whether or not a small number of holdings can be as diversified as the market as a whole—has an empirical answer. A small number of holdings can be *more* diversified than the market as a whole. The caveat is that we'd better be careful about which ones we pick. If we're as good as Buffett and Munger, then we'll have no problem. However, not many (if any) of us are that good. If you aren't, you might want to use broad index funds for the bulk of your portfolio and then hire Buffett and Munger for about one basis point annually (0.01 percent) via Berkshire Hathaway to provide some added diversification.

Anyway, it works for us.

Appendix B

Coping with Concentrated Holdings

For reasons good and bad, many investors have concentrated holdings. Perhaps you work for a company that force-feeds its company stock into your 401(k). Maybe you're a corporate officer with a nice option package who's expected to retain a hefty allocation of company stock for political reasons. Maybe dear old dad worked for General Electric all his life and left you with a pile of GE stock that's worth more than your house.

> **Q.** How do you deal with this 800-pound gorilla in the middle of your portfolio?
>
> **A.** Very carefully.

Your situation will undoubtedly be complicated enough to merit a sober conversation with your accountant before going off half-cocked into some half-baked investment scheme. In general, the smart move is to liquidate the big position. Individual stocks are volatile and typically don't compensate their owners for their added volatility, especially when compared with simply owning the market as a whole via an index fund. However, people avoid selling because they don't want to pay the enormous capital-gains taxes. If you're reading this before the year 2010 when the Bush tax cuts are clocked to expire, long-term federal capital-gains tax rates (15 percent) are as low as they've been in your lifetime and are very likely to be lower than they will be for lifetimes to come. Our advice: Sell before 2010 if it otherwise makes sense.

(If your concentrated holdings consist of appreciated company stock in a 401(k), the smart move might be to transfer it to an ordinary brokerage account, not to a rollover individual retirement account [IRA]. Once inside the IRA, the entire proceeds will come out as taxable income at your marginal tax rate. But if sold within a taxable brokerage account, you'll only pay for the cost basis of the stock at your marginal tax rate; the remainder is taxed as capital appreciation. The greater your appreciation and the higher your tax rate, the more you save using this strategy.)

Here's a typical scenario.

1. We recommend that a family sell its big stake in World Wide Widgets.

2. The family says, "Gee, we could never sell that World Wide Widgets stock that Pop left us. He worked there his whole life, you know. World Wide Widgets has been very good to this family. It would be disloyal."

3. World Wide Widgets falls 40 percent.

4. The family drops World Wide Widgets faster than Britney dropped Kevin Federline.

Moral: If you feel sentimental about a stock, it's important to ask yourself if you'd still feel that way if it were to decline in value by 40 percent.

This problem becomes more acute when you're currently working for the company where you also own the stock. In many cases, you can't sell without perturbing the political atmosphere governing your future; you don't want your name showing up in SEC filings. The stakes are high, because if the stock hits the skids, you might also get laid off—a double whammy. If you live in a company town and your house loses its value at the same time, it becomes a triple play, all at your expense.

For you high-net-worth types (and if you're dealing with this problem, you probably are), investment advisors will be eager to recommend using protective "puts" and covered "calls" to place a "collar" around your big position. Even if the transaction costs of the puts and calls offset each other, this will require ongoing and careful active management. You may rightly have some qualms about shorting your company stock. If you can't sell, this strategy becomes hard to implement, because you have to face the contingencies of possibly having it called away or putting it to others. It's a temporary solution at best because it locks your returns inside the collar.

There might be some other fancy things you could do—give the stock to your children, put it into a charitable remainder trust, put it into a limited partnership, and so on. But since this is a book on portfolio construction, let's look at what portfolio-structured solutions might work.

Our general strategy is going to be to flesh out the rest of the portfolio using the market sectors with the lowest correlation to the one with the concentrated position. The portfolio will be a doughnut around the big holding, which will fit into the hole.

How to Do It

Table B.1 shows the correlations of all the different market sectors with each other over the recent past. The QPP Monte Carlo software will allow us to make the exact calculations for the company we wish to diversify away from, but this is a start.

Table B.1: U.S. Market Sector Intercorrelations 2003–2006

	Materials	Retail	Cons. Cycl.	Cons. Stap.	Energy	Financial	Technology	Transportation	Utilities	Industrial
Materials (IYM)	100%									
Retail (RTH)	45%	100%								
Consumer Cyclic (XLY)	56%	86%	100%							
Consumer Staples (XLP)	26%	39%	46%	100%						
Energy (XLE)	60%	-2%	10%	-13%	100%					
Financial (XLF)	42%	48%	55%	42%	-13%	100%				
Technology (XLK)	58%	72%	81%	44%	17%	54%	100%			
Transportation (IYT)	64%	68%	75%	28%	20%	29%	64%	100%		
Utilities (XLU)	11%	-3%	5%	14%	27%	13%	6%	-16%	100%	
Industrial (XLI)	70%	62%	74%	39%	13%	45%	74%	84%	-14%	100%

Next, we have to determine how much risk we can afford. Using QPP, we can experiment with various allocations in our portfolio to see how they're likely to grow over time to fund our nest egg, which in turn will determine how much we can draw annually after we retire. Try a portfolio consisting of various mixes of the S&P 500 Index (VFINX) and short-term bonds (VBISX) as a quick method to determine the ratio of stocks to bonds that works best, and then write down the average annual expected returns and standard deviation of this portfolio as a reference point. If you have so much money that funding your retirement is a nonissue (lucky you!), then you can skip this step.

Example #1: International Paper

Let's assume for the sake of this example that we'll be trying to match a portfolio of 60 percent S&P 500 Index and 40 percent short-term bonds. This has a projected return of 8.2 percent against a standard deviation of 9.2 percent.

Enter the ticker of the company with the concentrated position into QPP, alongside the tickers from various market sector funds. For the sake of this example, let's assume we have a concentrated holding in International Paper (IP). We set the portfolio allocation to 100 percent IP, and then study the correlation table to see how the other market sectors correlate with it. The results are shown in Table B.2.

Table B.2: Correlations to International Paper		
Asset Class	Ticker	r
International Paper	IP	1.00
Materials	IYM	0.49
Retail	RTH	0.15
Consumer Cyclical	XLY	0.30
Consumer Staples	XLP	0.22
Energy	XLE	0.08
Finance	XLF	0.42
Industry	XLI	0.55
Utilities	XLU	-0.13
REITs	ICF	0.16
Commodities	^DJC	0.05
Malaysia	EWM	0.31
Japan	EWJ	0.30
Bonds	VBISX	-0.11

The lowest correlations seem to be energy (XLE), utilities (IDU) and commodities (^DJC). Of course, bonds (VBISX) have a low correlation to IP as well.

Let's assume that International Paper comprises 40 percent of our total holdings so that we have 60 percent of our portfolio left to allocate around it. Our goal is to bring the volatility level down to where it would have been with the generic 60/40 stock/bond portfolio, with (we hope) the same or better projected returns. To do this, we add, in equal measure, energy, utilities, and commodities—along with short-term bonds—until the standard deviation comes down to our targeted level, which was 9.2 percent. The resulting portfolio is shown in Figure B.1.

Figure B.1: Cutting International Paper

Fund Name	Percentage of Funds	Average Annual Return	Expected Annual Return	Expected Standard Deviation
IP	40.0%	11.84%	9.5%	9.2%
RTH	4.0%	10.34%		
XLE	4.0%	24.30%		
XLU	4.0%	12.71%		
^DJC	4.0%	17.69%		
VBISX	44.0%	4.93%		
–	0.0%	–		
–	0.0%	–		
–	0.0%	–		
–	0.0%	–		
–	0.0%	–		
–	0.0%	–		
–	0.0%	–		
–	0.0%	–		
–	0.0%	–		
–	0.0%	–		
–	0.0%	–		
–	0.0%	–		

Historical Data

Start: 12/31/2003	End: 12/31/2006
Average Annual Return	Standard Deviation (Annual)
2.1%	7.0%

Historical Beta: 57.3%
Historical Yield: 2.3%
Portfolio R^2: 31.8%

Performance of S&P 500 over historical period
Avg. Ann. Return S&P 500 (no dividends) 8.4%
Annual Standard Deviation on S&P 500 6.9%

This portfolio has the same standard deviation as the 60/40 stock/ bond portfolio, but expected returns of 9.5 percent versus 8.2 percent. Look at the "Historical Data" section in Figure B.1. This portfolio returned a little more than 2 percent annually for the past three years. Does this mean it's a failure? Quite the opposite: During this same time period, International Paper was down 14 percent. We told you that concentrated positions were risky! The portfolio buffered the loss beautifully.

At this point, we could go back to the retirement planning function of QPP and tweak the portfolio above until it gave us a better fit with our long-term goals. Since the expected returns are now slightly higher, we might be able to add more bonds for safety and still fund our nest egg. There's a lot of individual business risk with IP (or any concentrated holding), so the more we can do to contain the risk around it, the better.

Example #2: Microsoft

Let's assume that we're Seattle millionaires with Microsoft stock comprising 80 percent of our net worth. We have a tiger by the tail, a high volatility situation where the MSFT stock quote will stream across our computer screen so we can check it in the middle of the night to make sure we're still rich. This has the all the ingredients of a perfect storm. If we have such a huge stake captive, this means we must be current employees who will be at risk if Linux takes over the world. It probably means we live in Seattle, where we'll have trouble getting work as baristas at Starbucks if MSFT hits the skids. What should we do?

Let's begin by putting the usual tickers into QPP and pulling data back to 2000 so we expose ourselves to the full force of the previous downdraft. From 2000 through 2006, Microsoft delivered a minus 0.6 average annual return against a standard deviation of 37.2 percent. Going forward, the stock has an expected standard deviation of 39.4 percent.

How can we cope with this much volatility? If we put the remaining 20 percent of our money into short-term bonds, the portfolio's expected volatility comes down . . . to 31.4 percent. This is still Mr. Toad's Wild Ride. In a bad year, we stand to lose 44 percent of our money.

The correlation is shown in Table B.3

Table B.3: Correlations to Microsoft		
Asset Class	Ticker	r
Microsoft	MSFT	1.00
Consumer Cyclical	XLY	0.44
Consumer Staples	XLP	-0.01
Energy	XLE	0.13
Finance	XLF	0.25
Industry	XLI	0.38
Utilities	XLU	0.05
REITs	VGSIX	-0.02
Commodities	^DJC	-0.17
Malaysia	EWM	0.19
Japan	EWJ	0.31
Bonds	VBISX	-0.06

There are any number of funds we could employ that offer serious diversification, but they won't solve our volatility problem. We've already tried adding bonds, which have the lowest correlation of all, and even they haven't taken us as far as we want to go. This situation calls for more drastic measures.

For some years now, mutual fund companies have been offering "bear market" funds. These funds sell short, buy "put" options, and use leverage to achieve the opposite of what the index that they track does. For example, the Profunds UltraShort OTC Fund (ticker: USPIX) is designed to provide daily returns that (before expenses) correspond to twice the inverse of the NASDAQ 100 index, of which Microsoft is the crown jewel. Before expenses, to the extent this fund is successful in meeting its objective, if the NASDAQ is up 2 percent one day, this fund will be down 4 percent. If the NASDAQ is down 1 percent on any given day, this fund should be up 2 percent, and so on. In practice, expenses and tracking error will cause the fund to perform differently, but that's the general idea.

Over this same period we just looked at, the UltraShort OTC Fund had a correlation of minus .58 with the price movement of Microsoft. As extreme as it sounds, the best way to handle the Microsoft situation might be to put our remaining money into one of these bear markets funds.

These short funds confound the Monte Carlo simulator's internal risk-return blancing mechanism, so we're going to have to improvise. If the NASDAQ has an expected return of 19.3 percent, we might guesstimate that this amplified bear market fund has an inverse return of twice that, or minus 38.6 percent. So we adjust the dials accordingly. Figure B.2 shows the consequences.

The estimated future returns are undoubtedly quite inaccurate, but they're directionally correct. If Microsoft does well, the bear market fund will cut our returns considerably. But if Microsoft tanks, then USPIX should pull through, resucing us from financial oblivion. Under this scenario, a bad year might have us losing closer to 20 percent of our money instead of 47 percent if we hedge Microsoft with bonds.

There is no guarantee here, of course. It's possible that Microsoft might go in a sinkhole while the market as a whole goes up, in which case the strategy would backfire. It's also possible that the market might correct but Microsoft emerges unscathed, in which case we would have hit it big.

We cannot not act: We have to invest the available 20 percent of our portfolio in something. Our main goal is to trim the potential gargantuan losses stemming from our large individual stake. Using a bear market fund is a reasonable option.

Now get this: If, as is the most probable event, Microsoft has an okay year and USPIX goes down, we can sell USPIX at a loss. Then we can use this capital loss to offset the taxes on the sale of a like amount of MSFT, decreasing our outsized stake in that company. A few years of this could allow us to whittle down our concentrated position to a point where we can manage it without resorting to the dire contingency of shorting the market.

Figure B.2: Managing Microsoft

Fund Name	Percentage of Funds	Average Annual Return	Expected Annual Return	Expected Standard Deviation
MSFT	80.0%	22.30%	10.0%	21.2%
BONDS	0.0%	4.04%		
NASDAQ	0.0%	19.31%		
INV. NASDAQ X 2	20.0%	-38.62%		
-	0.0%	-		
-	0.0%	-		
-	0.0%	-		
-	0.0%	-		
-	0.0%	-		
-	0.0%	-		
-	0.0%	-		
-	0.0%	-		
-	0.0%	-		
-	0.0%	-		
-	0.0%	-		
-	0.0%	-		
-	0.0%	-		
-	0.0%	-		

Historical Data

	Expected Annual Return	Expected Standard Deviation
Start:	12/31/1999	End: 12/31/2006
Average Annual Return	0.9%	Standard Deviation (Annual) 24.6%

Historical Beta: 44.9%
Historical Yield: 2.1%
Portfolio R^2: 6.8%

Performance of S&P500 over historical period
Avg Ann Return S&P500 (no dividends) 0.5%
Annual Standard Deviation on S&P500 14.3%

There may even be a more targeted solution. Recently, ProShares has issued an UltraShort Technology ETF (ticker: REW). Instead of doing twice the reverse of the NASDAQ 100, this fund aims at twice the reverse of Dow Jones U.S. Technology Index. We couldn't get stats on this index back to 2000, but looking at two other technology indices (the AMEX Computer Technology Index and the CBOE Technology Index), we found correlations to Microsoft in the 60 to 70 percent range over this period. Putting the remainder of our portfolio into the ProShares UltraShort Technology ETF would probably lower the standard deviation even further.

Example #3: Valero Energy Corporation

Here's a fairly typical case: We have 15 percent of our liquid assets in a single stock—just enough to be a burr under the saddle. To make it tough on ourselves, let's say the stock is Valero Energy Corporation (VLO). Valero is wildly volatile: Its standard deviation over the past three years is close to 37 percent. How can we smooth it down?

Let's further assume that our baseline portfolio is the 60/40 S&P 500/short-term bond affair. Over the same period (2003–2006) this portfolio had a historical return of 9 percent against a very low standard deviation of 5 percent; it has an expected return of 8 percent against a standard deviation of 9 percent. Looking at QPP's value-at-risk calculator, we can estimate that this portfolio could be down 13 percent in a very bad year.

Imagine that we stuck with our initial allocation of 15 percent Valero and used just the S&P 500 and short-term bonds as our building blocks, trying to concoct a portfolio with no more volatility than the original 60/40 mix. We can make short work of this task: We have to throw away all our stocks and bet the farm on the bonds to squelch Valero's volatility. The results are shown in Table B.4.

Table B.4: Pouring Oil on Valero 2003–2006						
		HISTORICAL		EXPECTED		
Portfolio	Alloca-tion	Returns	S.D.	Returns	S.D.	Bad Year
Classic 60/40		9.4%	5.1%	8.1%	9.3%	-13.0%
S&P 500	60%					
Short-Term Bonds	40%					
15% Valero #1		9.7%	5.6%	9.5%	10.0%	-13.0%
Valero	15%					
S&P 500	0%					
Short-Term Bonds	85%					

Our portfolio has very slightly more volatility than before, even piling on all the bonds. Is there a better way?

Look back at Table B.1, which shows the intercorrelations among the various market sectors. Since Valero would fall squarely in "energy," we can see that two sectors have low correlations with it: finance and consumer staples. Adding 5 percent of each of these sectors works diversification magic. We can now add some S&P 500 back into the mix, and cook up the better returns shown in the Valero #2 portfolio in Table B.5.

Table B.5: Giving Valero a Lube Job 2003–2006						
		HISTORICAL		EXPECTED		
Portfolio	Alloca-tion	Returns	S.D.	Returns	S.D.	Bad Year
Classic 60/40		9.4%	5.1%	8.1%	9.3%	-13%
S&P 500	60%					
Short-Term Bonds	40%					
15% Valero #1		9.7%	5.6%	9.5%	10.0%	-13%
Valero	15%					
S&P 500	0%					
Short-Term Bonds	85%					
15% Valero #2		12.4%	5.6%	10.7%	10.4%	-13%
Valero	15%					
S&P 500	15%					
Short-Term Bonds	60%					
Financial	5%					
Consumer Staples	5%					

This new portfolio preserves the 15 percent obligatory Valero allocation but now uses consumer staples stocks (ticker: XLP) for the bulk of the equities. At the price of imperceptibility greater expected monthly volatility, we purchase 28 percent better expected annual returns—12.4 percent versus 9.5 percent.

In Sum

Only a masochist likes to write a fat capital-gains check to "United States Treasury." Nevertheless, it's probably the smart move, especially if you can do so before the Bush tax cuts expire. If you can't liquidate your concentrated position and exchange it for a diversified portfolio, one alternative is to build a compensating portfolio as a buffer around it.

Glossary

Beta: A measure of the sensitivity of the price movements of a security or portfolio to movements in the stock market as a whole (typically, the S&P 500 index). An S&P 500 index fund will have a beta of close to 100 percent. A stock with a beta greater than one (a technology stock, perhaps) amplifies within itself the price movements of the larger stock market, while a stock with a beta of less than one (a utility stock, perhaps) will be less responsive to those same movements.

Correlation: The extent to which two things vary together. It's measured by a *correlation coefficient* that can range from +1 (a perfect positive correlation) to 0 (no correlation) to -1 (a perfect negative correlation). Two airline stocks might have a high positive correlation with each other because all the general factors affecting the industry affect both of them, but they might have no correlation with the performance of stocks in the drug industry and a negative correlation with stocks in the oil industry. (One of the airlines' biggest costs is fuel. So when oil is expensive, energy stocks might be up, while the earnings for airlines will be depressed and their stocks might be down.) The importance for investors is that by holding assets whose price swings have as low a correlation with each other as possible, the standard deviation of the portfolio will be suppressed (since one will be up while the other is down), yielding better risk-adjusted returns.

Efficient frontier: The set of portfolios whose allocations are per-fectly optimized to offer the highest returns for a specific amount of risk or standard deviation. This frontier can only be known historically. Monte Carlo simulation is a tool for creating forward-looking portfolios that lie closer to this ideal than typically can be created just by copying the portfolios that achieved it in the past.

Efficient market hypothesis: The view (originating with Eugene Fama) that financial markets efficiently incorporate all available histori-cal and anticipated information into the prices of the securities. The implication is that technical and fundamental analysis can't improve individual stock picking, since everything that's known about a stock has already been built into the price by the rational, competing, profit-maximizing agents who are buying and selling it in the information-transparent market.

Index investing: The proposition (often linked to the efficient market hypothesis) that investors are better served simply buying low-expense mutual funds or exchange-traded funds that broadly mimic the performance of stock indexes like the S&P 500 Index or the MSCI Europe, Australia, and Far East Index. Index investors believe that active management (which attempts to outperform the broad market indexes via individual stock picking, short-term market timing, momentum strategies, behavioral strategies, and the like) add negative utility after expenses.

Mean: The arithmetic *average* of all scores, calculated by adding all the scores together and dividing by the number of scores. The *histori-cal mean return* is the average annual return that your portfolio would have received over the period sampled. The *expected mean return* is the Monte Carlo simulator's estimate of the forward-looking annual returns from the same portfolio.

The expected mean return differs from the historical mean return for two reasons. First, it takes into account the program's risk-return bal-ancing, which attempts to align the risks and returns of the constituent assets with long-term expectations about the relationship between risk and return in capital markets. Second, the historical returns represent one scenario that did occur. The expected future returns represent the average of thousands of possible future scenarios that might occur. We don't know which future will come true, so it should be considered a reasonable estimate—one that's likely to be better than just projecting the historical returns into the future.

Modern Portfolio Theory: The view that investors should analyze their portfolios as a whole (and not just as the sum of individual securities), composed with the aim of maximizing their risk-adjusted returns in the service of achieving their portfolios' objectives.

Monte Carlo simulation: A technique for modeling the future behavior of a portfolio by using a computer's random number generator to populate numerous hypothetical future sets of investment returns based upon the expected means, standard deviations, and intercorrelations of the portfolio's weighted components, and then measuring where the resulting returns cluster. The technique became accessible to the retail investor with the development of the personal computer. It became especially useful for its ability to simulate cash flows at the same time, such that it can model the funding and withdrawal from a retirement account over many years and estimate the probability of achieving a successful solution.

R-squared: A measure of the variance of a portfolio that's explained by movements in the larger market (the S&P 500). It's also called the *coefficient of determination*. The value can range from 0 to 100. If zero, the portfolio's price fluctuations are completely independent from those of the stock market—such as might be desirable for a hedge fund, for example. If 100, then the portfolio's price movements are completely explained by the stock market as a whole.

Standard deviation: A measure of the dispersion of scores around the mean. If you must know, it's calculated by taking the square root of the variance, which is the sum of the squared deviations of each individual score from the mean. When scores follow a normally distributed bell-shaped curve, the standard deviation allows us to estimate how far the returns will depart from the mean. The returns should fall within one standard deviation 68 percent of the time; and 95 percent of the time, they should fall within two standard deviations of the mean. In practice, outlying investment returns—for good and especially for ill— are more likely to occur than this.

The *historical standard deviation* measures the annual volatility that actually occurred over the time period sampled. The *expected standard deviation* estimates the portfolio's projected standard deviation going into the future. Standard deviations of returns tend to be more robust than the means of returns. Nonetheless, the expected standard deviation can differ from the historical standard deviation due to the QPP Monte Carlo simulator's internal risk-return balancing and also because the future standard deviation is measured from looking at the dispersion of thousands of possible sets of returns from the mean, while the historical standard deviation describes one data set.

In general, capital markets pay long-term investors proportionately to the burden of standard deviation that they assume. Short-term investors need to avoid assets with a high standard deviation since they may have to liquidate their positions when the prices have fluctuated downward. Long-term investors, however, can afford to ride out the short-term fluctuations of high standard deviation assets in pursuit of their higher long-term projected returns. The goal of portfolio planning is to use diversification to secure the maximum expected returns for the minimum expected risk in meeting the portfolio's objectives.

Index

The letters *f* and *t* following page numbers refer to figures and tables respectively.

About the Authors

 **Ben Stein** can be seen talking about finance on Fox TV news every week and writing about it regularly in *The New York Times* Sunday Business section and on Yahoo! Finance. No wonder: Not only is he the son of the world-famous economist and government advisor Herbert Stein, but Ben is a respected economist in his own right. He received his B.A. with honors in economics from Columbia University in 1966, studied economics in the graduate school of economics at Yale while he earned his law degree there, and worked as an economist for the Department of Commerce.

Ben Stein is known to many as a movie and television personality, especially from *Ferris Bueller's Day Off* and from his long-running quiz show, *Win Ben Stein's Money*. But he has probably worked more in personal and corporate finance than anything else. He has written about finance for *Barron's* and *The Wall Street Journal* for decades. He was one of the chief busters of the junk-bond frauds of the 1980s, has been a longtime critic of corporate executives' self-dealing, and has co-written eight self-help books about personal finance. He frequently travels the country speaking about finance in both serious and humorous ways, and is a regular contributor to the *CBS News Sunday Morning* and Fox News Network.

Website: **www.benstein.com**

Phil DeMuth was the valedictorian of his class at the University of California at Santa Barbara in 1972, then took his master's in communications and Ph.D. in clinical psychology. Both a psychologist and an investment adviser, Phil has written for *The Wall Street Journal, Barron's,* the *Louis Rukeyser Newsletter,* the *Journal of Financial Planning,* and

forbes.com, as well as *Human Behavior* and *Psychology Today.* He has co-written (with Ben Stein) five books on investing and personal finance. His opinions have been quoted in **theStreet.com**, *Yahoo! Finance, On Wall Street,* and *Fortune* magazine, and he has been profiled in *Research* magazine and seen on *Forbes on Fox* and *Wall Street Week* as well as CNBC's *On the Money, Squawk Box,* and *Closing Bell.* He is managing director of Conservative Wealth Management LLC in Los Angeles, a registered investment advisor to high-net-worth individuals and foundations.

Website: **www.phildemuth.com**

N B P

We hope you enjoyed this book.
If you'd like additional information, please contact
New Beginnings Press through their distributors:

Hay House, Inc.
P.O. Box 5100
Carlsbad, CA 92018-5100

(760) 431-7695 or **(800) 654-5126**
(760) 431-6948 (fax) or **(800) 650-5115 (fax)**
www.hayhouse.com® • **www.hayfoundation.org**

Distributed in Australia by: Hay House Australia Pty. Ltd. • 18/36 Ralph St.
Alexandria NSW 2015 • *Phone:* 612-9669-4299 • *Fax:* 612-9669-4144
www.hayhouse.com.au

Distributed in the United Kingdom by: Hay House UK, Ltd.
292B Kensal Rd., London W10 5BE • *Phone:* 44-20-8962-1230
Fax: 44-20-8962-1239 • www.hayhouse.co.uk

Distributed in the Republic of South Africa by: Hay House SA (Pty), Ltd.,
P.O. Box 990, Witkoppen 2068 • *Phone/Fax:* 27-11-467-8904
orders@psdprom.co.za • www.hayhouse.co.za

Distributed in India by: Hay House Publishers India, Muskaan Complex,
Plot No. 3, B-2, Vasant Kunj, New Delhi 110 070 • *Phone:* 91-11-4176-1620
Fax: 91-11-4176-1630 • www.hayhouse.co.in

Distributed in Canada by: Raincoast • 9050 Shaughnessy St.,
Vancouver, B.C. V6P 6E5 • *Phone:* (604) 323-7100 • *Fax:* (604) 323-2600

Tune in to **HayHouseRadio.com®** for the best in inspirational talk radio featuring
top Hay House authors! And, sign up via the Hay House USA Website to receive the
Hay House online newsletter and stay informed about what's going on with your
favorite authors. You'll receive bimonthly announcements about: Discounts and
Offers, Special Events, Product Highlights, Free Excerpts, Giveaways, and more!
www.hayhouse.com®